DISCARD

D1379487

Also by the Author

The Erin O'Reilly Mysteries
Black Velvet
Irish Car Bomb
White Russian
Double Scotch
Manhattan (coming soon)

The Clarion Chronicles
Ember of Dreams

Double Scotch

The Erin O'Reilly Mysteries
Book Four

Steven Henry

Clickworks Press • Baltimore, MD

Copyright © 2018 Steven Henry
Cover design © 2018 Ingrid Henry
Cover photo used under license from iStockPhoto.com (Credit:
quavondo/iStockPhoto)
NYPD shield photo used under license from Shutterstock.com (Credit: Stephen
Mulcahey/Shutterstock)
Author photo © 2017 Shelley Paulson Photography
Spine image used under license from iStockPhoto.com (Credit: gresei/iStockPhoto)
All rights reserved

First publication: Clickworks Press, 2018
Release: CWP-EOR4-INT-H.IS-1.0

Sign up for updates, deals, and exclusive sneak peeks at clickworkspress.com/join.

ISBN-10: 1-943383-47-2
ISBN-13: 978-1-943383-47-4

This is a work of fiction. Names, characters, places, organizations, and events are
either the products of the author's imagination or used in a fictitious manner. Any
resemblance to actual persons, living or dead, is purely coincidental.

For all the real life K-9 officers and their partners.

Double Scotch on the Rocks

Place ice cubes in a whiskey glass.
Pour 3 oz. Scotch whiskey over ice. Serve.

Chapter 1

"Rolf! *Fass!*" Erin O'Reilly snapped.

Her partner sprang into action. His feet barely touched the ground as he charged. The perp didn't try to run. That was smart; Rolf was faster than any man in New York. Instead, the poor guy threw his arm out in front of himself.

Rolf had him. His teeth snapped shut on the man's arm. With a terrific snarl, all ninety pounds of German Shepherd piled into the guy. As Rolf drove his target in a stumbling backward sprawl, the dog's tail wagged enthusiastically. He was having a great time.

"Okay! Okay!" the victim said. "I give up!"

"Rolf! *Pust!*" Erin ordered, giving the command in the dog's native German. Rolf obediently let go of the man's sleeve and returned to Erin's side, tail still wagging. "Good boy," she said, holding out his favorite rubber Kong ball. Rolf immediately clamped his teeth on the toy and began happily gnawing at it.

"Good boy?" Vic Neshenko echoed, brushing at the sleeve of his bite-suit. "He almost bit clean through."

"Sure," Erin said, watching her K-9 play. "You're supposed to feel it. If he doesn't bite hard, then what's the point?"

"I got an idea," her fellow detective said. "Next time, you wear the suit, I'll give the orders. We'll see how you like that."

"I've been in the suit," she said. "K-9 school, everybody wears the suit sometimes, to help the other guys train their dogs."

"Like Tasers," Vic muttered. "Gotta ride the lightning before they let you carry 'em."

"At least they don't have the same rule for sidearms," Erin said.

That shut both of them up for a minute. It had been almost a month since their gunfight at JFK Airport. Erin and Vic had both killed men that night. They'd been clean shootings—as clean as taking a life could be—but it was something neither of them really wanted to talk about.

Now they were in Central Park, taking advantage of an unseasonably cool late-July day to get some outdoor training done. Erin worked Rolf every day, but she was the one person on earth he would never bite, so she needed to partner up for bite-work. Vic hadn't exactly jumped at the opportunity, but Vic wasn't jumping at anything these days. His bullet wounds had healed nicely, so that he hardly limped at all, but his spirit had taken a beating.

Erin worried about him. Vic had always been a surly guy, but since their last case, he'd been downright unpleasant. She knew why. It was his girlfriend. Ex-girlfriend, of course. When a girl set a guy up to be killed, it put a lot of stress on the relationship. Even though it hadn't been the girl's idea, or her choice, and she'd tried to walk it back, the experience had left Detective Neshenko with an even worse view of human nature than he'd had before.

Erin wanted to help him, but wasn't sure how. Hell, she had her own issues. The first week after the shootings, she'd had nightmares every single night. She kept waking up in a cold sweat, seeing muzzle flashes in the dark, grabbing for her Glock automatic in the nightstand. At least she hadn't shot any holes in her ceiling. Thank God for good trigger discipline. The dreams had spaced themselves out lately, and her temper wasn't flaring up like it had, but she knew she wasn't quite herself yet.

"It's been quiet," she said to fill the silence. "That's something." Their Major Crimes unit hadn't had anything on their plate for nearly a week. That was one reason Lieutenant Webb hadn't objected to them taking some time out of the office.

"Great," Vic said. "Just fantastic."

"What?" she said. "You tired of moping around, ready to get off the bench?"

"I don't mope," Vic said.

"What do you call it, then?"

"I'm Russian," he said. "We brood."

He smiled. Just a little, but it was a smile, and that was progress. Maybe there was hope for him.

"You hoping we catch a case?" she asked.

"Beats being a chew-toy," he said. "I'm sick of sitting around doing nothing."

Rolf, realizing Erin's distraction, stopped chewing on his ball. He held it in his mouth and stared over it at Erin. His tail went back and forth in a slow, hopeful wave.

Erin's phone buzzed in her pocket. "*Pust!*" she ordered Rolf, who dropped his toy at once. She fished out the phone and saw Webb's name on the screen.

"O'Reilly," she said.

"You got Neshenko with you?" her commanding officer asked.

"Most of him."

"Okay, the two of you get down to Corlears Hook Park," Webb said.

"What've we got?" she asked.

"Looks like a double homicide," he said.

"On our way," Erin said, disconnecting. She looked at Vic. "Looks like you got your wish. Time to go back to work."

*   *   *

Corlears Hook lay on the southeastern edge of Manhattan, on the bank of the East River. By the time Vic, Erin, and Rolf arrived, in Erin's brand-new unmarked police Charger, the uniforms had established a perimeter of yellow tape. Half a dozen officers were there, along with a couple of unnecessary paramedics who were finishing packing up their gear.

Detective Kira Jones waved them over to the shoreline. She'd recently re-dyed her hair, a habit picked up from her days as a liaison with the gang task force. Its tips were a bright, electric blue that made it easy to pick her out of a crowd.

"Where's the LT?" Erin asked.

"With Levine," Jones said, gesturing with her thumb. "We just got here."

Sarah Levine was the Medical Examiner. She and Lieutenant Webb were standing near the water's edge, staring at a couple of lumpy shapes wedged in among the rocks. Levine was wearing a white lab coat, wire-rimmed glasses, and a thoughtful expression. Webb had his hands on his hips and a cigarette clamped in the corner of his mouth.

"What've we got, sir?" Erin asked, stepping carefully on the slippery stones. Rolf, catching the scent, alerted her to the presence of a dead body.

"Two victims," Webb said. He took the cigarette from his mouth and used it as a pointer. "Jogger saw the crows going at them, wondered what was there."

"Where's the runner?" Vic asked.

"Going over her statement," Webb said, cocking his head. "She didn't see much. As soon as she figured out she was looking at bodies, she called it in."

Erin peered past Levine at the bodies. She couldn't make out much. "What do you think, Doc?" she asked.

Levine didn't look at her. "They were washed up here," the ME said. "This isn't where they died."

"Two bodies, washed up together?" Erin said. "That happen often?"

"Depends on the currents," Levine said. "I'll need to look at the charts."

"What are the chances they're related?" Erin said.

"Won't know till I do the bloodwork," Levine said. "They're both adult males, so it's possible they might be brothers."

"What I meant is," Erin said, "are we looking at separate incidents?"

"Unlikely," Levine said. "Judging from the condition of the bodies, they probably went into the water at about the same time. My best estimate, until I study them further, is that they died within the last twenty-four hours, probably between ten and midnight."

"Accident, or foul play?" Erin asked.

"Check the hands," Vic said, entering the conversation.

Erin followed his look. The body he was examining was face-down. Its hands were secured with a cheap plastic zip-tie.

"Tied up," Webb said. "Definitely homicide."

Erin bent over to see more closely. "There's something wrong with that hand," she said.

"All five fingernails have been torn off," Levine said.

"Could that have been caused by something in the water?" Erin asked. She thought she knew the answer already, but was hoping to hear different.

The other three all shook their heads. "Torture," Vic muttered.

"Preliminary cause of death is a single gunshot wound to the back of the cranium," Levine said. "Probably a handgun, thirty-eight caliber, maybe nine-millimeter."

"And the other victim?" Webb asked.

"The other body presents identically," Levine said. "The hands are secured behind the back, a single gunshot wound to the head. The only difference is that both hands on the second one are intact."

"Tied up, interrogated, and executed," Webb said. He rubbed the bridge of his nose. "Then chucked into the river. We know where they came from?"

"Again, I'll need to check a chart of the currents," Levine said with a touch of annoyance.

"Could've come from anywhere," Vic said. "Bridge, boat, whatever."

"You got all the pictures you need?" Webb asked Levine. One of the ME's lab-techs was snapping shots of the corpses from every possible angle.

"Not quite," Levine said. "We need a few more minutes."

"Okay, get them out of the water as soon as you're done," he said. "We need IDs on them ASAP. And I want you back in the lab right away."

Levine gave him a curious look. "Where else would I go?"

He sighed. "Never mind. I want you to double-check cause of death. Get me a bullet, if the rounds didn't exit the skulls. Print 'em, check dental records. And get started on the clothes, see if we've got fibers, chemicals, anything that didn't wash out in the river."

Levine's annoyance was becoming more obvious. "Lieutenant, I do several examinations every week," she said. "I have a medical doctorate."

"Okay, okay," Webb said, holding up his hands. "I just want you to move this one to the head of the line. Anything you can tell us will help."

"How cold was it last night?" Erin broke in. She was still looking at the bodies.

"Seventy-five, give or take," Jones said. "Why?"

"These guys are dressed pretty warm," Erin said. Both dead men were clad in wool sweaters, one gray, one dark green. The body on the left also had a watch cap on his head. The bullet hole had entered his skull just below its edge.

"Yeah," Webb said. "Sailors, you think?"

"Looks like it," Vic said.

"That raises a question of jurisdiction," Jones said.

"Our bodies, our problem," Vic said.

"We're Major Crimes," Webb reminded Jones. "It doesn't matter where the body came from."

"It matters if they were on a ship over the Jersey border," Jones said. "The state line runs through the harbor, and depending on where the boat was at the time they were killed, if we can even figure that out. Of course, it's probably a Port Authority matter in any case..."

"Oh, for Christ's sake," Vic said.

"Until we know where they came from, they're ours," Webb said. "You really want to worry about that bureaucratic bullshit now?"

"I thought that was your job, sir," Erin said with false innocence.

"May you make Lieutenant someday," Webb said. "And may you on that day be blessed with detectives of your own, just like you."

"I bet he says the same thing to his kids," Jones said out of the side of her mouth.

"Not much of a crime scene," Vic said. "This is just where they fetched up."

"I agree," Webb said. "But we'll need the CSU guys to comb the rocks anyway, in case any other evidence washed up."

They all took a moment to look at the shoreline. Empty bottles, plastic bags, and all sorts of trash were scattered everywhere. If there was anything relevant, it would be a needle in a haystack of random litter. Jones said what each of them was thinking.

"Those poor bastards."

Chapter 2

Until Levine started getting her lab work done, there wasn't a lot for the detectives to do. No IDs, no cell phones. They ran the fingerprints right away, of course, but got no matches in the NYPD database. Jones ran the prints by the FBI and Homeland Security, just to be thorough, and came up empty there, too.

The clothes were something to go on, so that was where Vic and Erin started. The two dead men had been wearing sweaters and trousers, one pair of slacks, one pair of corduroys, brown leather shoes, turtleneck shirts, and one watch cap. The lab needed to check for fibers that might've been transferred from the perp, but in the meantime, they had the clothing labels.

"Ghillie Brogues?" Vic said, looking at the pictures the CSU guys had snapped of the first man's shoes. "The hell kind of a name is that? Look, they say 'Thistle' on the bottom. That sound like something you want on your feet?"

"They also say 'Scotland,'" Erin pointed out. She went to her computer and quickly found that Ghillie Brogues could be bought in the UK or in America. Or anywhere at all, thanks to the Internet. "Maybe these guys are from Britain. Nice looking shoes."

Vic shrugged. "Basic guy's shoe."

"Not exactly a sailor's shoe," Erin said. They looked more like dress shoes to her, and there wasn't enough tread for them to be practical for shipboard wear.

Vic shrugged again. He didn't seem too interested.

Erin didn't have the patience to deal with his sulking. She checked the shoe sizes and noted them down, then moved on to the other clothing. All of it had been made in the British Isles. She duly put that information up on the department whiteboard. Next to the photos of the dead men, she wrote "British/Scottish?"

Webb wandered over. "Got anything?" he asked.

"Yeah," Vic said. "Erin's got it narrowed down to about ten million suspects."

"No suspects yet," she said. "Not even close to an ID. But I think we should see about ships coming over from the UK."

"Erin," Jones called over, "do you have any idea how much cargo comes through the harbor?"

"Not really," Erin said, with a sinking feeling that she was about to find out.

"The port handled about three million incoming cargo containers," Jones said. "Last year alone. Going out, another three million, give or take."

"How much of that from Britain?" Webb asked.

"Port Authority would have the exact numbers," Jones said, working her keyboard. "But two and a half percent of the imports come from the United Kingdom. Four percent of the exports head there. So that works out to... let's see... about seventy-five thousand containers coming in, and a hundred and twenty K going out. Roughly."

"You should've been an accountant," Vic said. "Why are you a cop?"

Jones shrugged. "Follow the money. That's what I've always heard about solving cases."

"That's gotta be a lot of ships," Erin said.

"Between one and two hundred a day," Jones said. "Figure maybe a dozen to or from the UK."

"That's manageable," Webb said. "Jones, get on the phone to the Port Authority. I want a list of those ships, for the last three days."

"That's not counting passenger ships," Jones said. "Of course, there aren't many true passenger liners these days, but lots of ships carry passengers. Just because these guys are wearing clothes from Britain doesn't mean—"

"I know that," Webb said. "But it's a place to start. Neshenko, put in a request to Interpol for a check on these prints. If they're European, they may have records overseas."

"What should I do?" Erin asked.

"I think maybe—" Webb began, but she never found out what he was going to say. His phone rang mid-sentence. The Lieutenant held up a hand as he fished out the phone and answered. "Webb."

He listened a moment. "Understood," he said. "I'll send someone." He disconnected and stared at the phone for a moment without saying anything else.

"What's going on, sir?" Erin asked.

"We've got another one," he sighed.

"Another body?" Jones asked.

He nodded.

"Where'd this one wash up?" Vic wondered.

"It didn't," Webb said. "It's unrelated. We've got a female found locked in a hotel room."

"Suicide?" Vic said.

"They wouldn't have called us for a suicide," Jones said.

"Probably not," Webb agreed. "O'Reilly, get over to the DoubleTree. This one's yours."

"What about the other two bodies?" she asked.

"We're Major Crimes," Webb said. "That doesn't always mean one crime at a time. We'll keep working these two, you see what you can turn up on the new one. We'll compare notes. Go."

Police work often required officers to shift gears on short notice. Erin had been on the force too long to be badly thrown by it. "Will do," she said, grabbing her K-9's leash. "*Hier*, Rolf."

*   *   *

Erin pulled up to the front of the hotel in her Charger. She was still enjoying the new-car smell. Her last car had been totaled near the end of her previous case. If a good partner was one who'd take a bullet for her, then that car had been a very good partner indeed, absorbing enough rifle rounds that the guys at the repair lot had just shaken their heads and told her to put in the paperwork for a replacement. She'd only had the new car for a week, and it handled like a dream.

She parked in the police space. There was no sign of other officers out front. She got out of the car and took a deep breath, feeling the weight of her vest. She'd been wearing body armor under her outer clothes on duty ever since the gunfights with the Russians. Department regulations didn't absolutely require it for plainclothes work, and in late summer it was heavy and uncomfortable, but she didn't care. Every time she thought she might leave it behind, she remembered seeing AK rounds punching holes in her windshield. She'd taken to carrying a backup gun, too; a five-shot revolver in an ankle holster.

Rolf was another matter. The poor dog couldn't even sweat, so if she didn't think there was a chance of trouble, she left his armor off. She didn't feel quite right about that, but sometimes there just wasn't a right decision to be made.

A foot patrolman was in the lobby, standing at the front desk with the manager. The hotel's guy was skinny and nervous, with a sorry little mustache that looked as unhappy as its owner.

Erin squared her shoulders and walked up to the desk. This was her first time flying solo as a detective. The uniform glanced at her without much interest and turned back to the manager.

"You were saying, sir?" he prompted.

Erin bristled. She flipped out her shield. "Detective O'Reilly, Major Crimes," she said. "What's the situation?"

The patrolman did a double-take. He looked her over with the slow scan that too many male officers gave to a female cop, especially a good-looking one. Erin let his gaze slide off her. She'd done this dance too many times to be too bothered by it.

"When you're ready, Officer," she said coolly.

He cleared his throat, having the decency to be a little embarrassed. "Right. I'm Barton. Hickman—that's my partner— and I took the call. The maid found something when she was doing the rooms. Door was locked. She knocked and called, got no answer, and got worried. Hotel security spooked and phoned it in. We figured maybe a 10-54C, so we made entry."

The code Barton had used indicated a potential ambulance case, cardiac arrest. "You kicked in the door?" Erin asked.

"Had to," Barton said with a shrug. "Night lock was engaged."

"Sir, madam, please," the manager said, waving his hands in agitation. "Can we perhaps discuss this in a more, ah, discreet location?"

Erin glanced around the room. They were certainly attracting attention. A half-dozen spectators in the lobby were watching them. One, a teenage boy, was filming with his phone.

She'd probably be a minor Internet star on his social-media page by the end of the day.

"Why don't we go up to the room, sir," she suggested. "Officer Barton, is Hickman there now?"

"Yeah," Barton said. "He's securing the scene."

"Did you call for a bus?" she asked as they got on the elevator.

Barton shook his head. "She was cold when we got there."

"What can you tell me about her?"

"It's a chick. I mean, a girl. That is, a young woman." Barton was getting flustered.

"I know what a chick is, Barton," she said.

The elevator started rising. She noted there was a security camera in it. "Do those work?" she asked the manager.

"Yes, yes," he said. "They are a closed-circuit, ah, system. The film runs to the, ah, security station."

"I'll need the recordings," she said.

The elevator stopped at the fourteenth floor which, Erin reflected, was really the thirteenth, in that weird architect superstition. It was obvious room 1410 was the right one. The door was closed, but another NYPD patrolman was standing opposite with his arms crossed, leaning against the wall. He straightened up when he saw them and gave Erin a once-over.

"O'Reilly, Major Crimes," she said, walking up to the door and pulling on a pair of disposable rubber gloves from the roll she kept in a pocket. "You've been inside?"

"Yeah," Hickman said. "But we didn't touch anything."

"Except the victim," she prompted.

"Well, yeah," he said. "But just to check her vitals."

"And you were certain she was dead?"

"Yeah," Hickman said.

"Certain enough you didn't call a bus?"

"Yeah." Apparently that was his favorite word.

Erin braced herself. If there was any chance the victim had still been alive, proper procedure would've been to call an ambulance. That they hadn't bothered suggested this was going to be a messy one. Maybe the girl's head was lying on the bedside table or something. She'd seen some pretty screwed-up things in her time with Patrol. She took a breath. "Okay," she said and carefully opened the door.

The first thing that hit her was the smell. She'd been expecting the smell of death; blood and other body fluids, mixed with that sickly-sweet scent that was hard to describe but impossible to forget. What she got instead was perfume. It was a heavy, rich scent, so strong she could almost see it in the air, like a crimson haze. Rolf snorted and sneezed. Under ordinary circumstances, Erin would've found it a pleasant smell, if maybe a little heavy and sensual. Not a scent she'd wear herself.

The room was a little small for the king-size bed that took up most of the space. A window on the far wall looked out over the river. There was a desk-unit on the opposite wall from the bed, with a rolling chair, a coffeemaker under the TV, and a wine bottle and cut-glass goblet on top of it. And on the bed lay the victim.

Erin had never seen a tidier crime scene—if that was even what it was. A pretty blonde lay on top of the neatly-made bed. No, not pretty, Erin thought. She was beautiful. Her hair was carefully styled, resting in golden waves on the pillow. She wore a black cocktail dress, brand-new from the look of it and cut to show off a very attractive figure, with black nylons and high-heeled black shoes. Her hands were clasped on her stomach. A bouquet of red roses was gripped in her fingers. The flowers hadn't started to wilt yet.

Erin walked across the room, taking care not to touch or disturb anything. Up close, she could see the woman was wearing makeup, a full, professional job. The lipstick was bright red and looked freshly-applied.

Nonetheless, the woman was obviously dead. Even under the lipstick, Erin could see the bluish tint to the lips. There was no sign of breath or movement. She checked for a pulse anyway. Nothing.

The two patrolmen were standing in the doorway. She could feel them watching her. "This how you found her?" she asked.

"Yeah," Hickman predictably replied.

"You said the night-lock was engaged?" she asked Barton.

He pointed to the part of the door in question. It was an old-style chain that could be slid into place as an extra safeguard. More to the point, it was operated from the inside, not the outside, of the room. It was broken now, hanging by a loose screw.

"You clear the bathroom?"

"Yeah," Hickman said.

Erin checked it anyway, having formed a low impression of Hickman's personal initiative. It was empty, except for a black faux-leather purse by the sink. She looked in the purse, hoping for ID.

She got more than she bargained for. In addition to a cosmetic kit, a packet of condoms, a roll of breath mints, and some keys, she found a billfold. Inside it was some cash, a driver's license for Penelope Jackson, and another driver's license in the name Jennifer Paxton. Both licenses showed the same face, a face matching the one on the body cooling in the next room.

"Son of a bitch," Erin muttered.

"What?" Barton asked, poking his head into the bathroom.

"Never mind," she said, replacing the billfold exactly as she'd found it. She was glad to see the money. She'd heard of uniforms responding to crime scenes and pocketing any loose cash they found lying around. The bills still being there meant these two probably hadn't rifled the scene.

Erin went back outside and looked over the desk. The wine bottle was bothering her. She crouched and stared at it. Hotel-brand red wine, nothing too fancy. The cork was in it, but it had obviously been opened and re-corked. She could smell the wine if she got close, even over the perfume. The glass next to the bottle had a little bit of wine still at the bottom.

"She had a drink," Erin said to herself. "Then... what? She lay down on the bed, without taking her shoes off, and died?"

That didn't make any sense. She shook her head and closed her eyes, doing a trick her dad had taught her. Slowly, she opened them again, taking the scene in again as if for the first time.

She saw Rolf sniffing at a patch of carpet next to the bed. That carpet section was darker than the others. Erin stepped quickly forward and dropped down to take a closer look. At first she thought it was a bloodstain, which also didn't make any sense. The girl on the bed didn't have a mark on her. Then she realized it was a wine spill. Maybe the girl hadn't had her drink after all. It was the only thing in the room that indicated any sort of struggle.

Erin's first look at the scene was over. She'd need CSU to take a look at this. And she'd need Levine. The Medical Examiner was going to have a busy couple of days. Erin got on her radio and called Dispatch to send the reinforcements. She hoped they'd find something, because at the moment, she didn't have the slightest idea what had happened here.

Her first solo scene investigation, and it was a genuine locked-room mystery.

Chapter 3

When Levine got to the scene, Erin was still trying to figure what had happened. Penelope Jackson—or Jennifer Paxton—was twenty-two years old, or twenty-three, depending on which fake ID she believed. Both were fakes, she was sure of that. Reasonably good ones, but still fake. She'd checked out plenty of licenses in her time on Patrol, and knew the look and feel of a real one.

The ME came in, glanced around, and approached the body. She didn't say anything to Erin. Since the corpse was in plain view, there was clearly nothing the detective needed to tell her.

"Sorry for the extra work," Erin offered.

"What do you mean?" Levine asked, bending over the victim.

"That's number three today," Erin said.

"So?"

"What can you tell me?" she asked, giving up on small talk.

"Probably cyanide poisoning," Levine said.

"You sure?"

"I wouldn't say 'probably' if I was sure. I'd say I was sure."

"Right," Erin said, determined to play nice. "Why do you think so?"

"Cyanosis on the lips," Levine said. "You can see it under the lipstick. Classic oxygen deprivation. Cyanide prevents tissues from utilizing oxygen in the bloodstream."

"What else could've caused it?"

Levine shrugged. "Asphyxiation. Carbon monoxide, maybe. Strangulation."

"Not strangulation," Erin said.

"No ligature marks," Levine agreed. She gently opened one of the victim's eyes partway with a gloved fingertip. "No hemorrhage in the eyeball. Poisoning or oxygen deprivation. Probably poison."

"This room's not airtight," Erin said. "Someone could've piped gas through the vents."

"The building has central air," Levine said.

"They'd have gassed half the floor, then," Erin said. "How much cyanide would you need to kill someone?"

"Not much if it's a gas, but it's lighter than air. You need a sealed environment for it to be really effective."

"What if it was eaten or injected?"

"At least ten milligrams," Levine said. "But to be sure, you need a couple hundred. Even then, ingested cyanide takes several minutes to kill, maybe up to half an hour. It's usually self-administered."

"Suicide," Erin said.

"Usually." Levine agreed.

Erin looked at the room again. "We'll need to test the wine bottle."

"Bloodwork will show poisoning," Levine said.

"Suicide," Erin muttered, trying on the theory. If Jennifer, or Penelope, had decided to kill herself by poison, she very well could've staged the scene. Get the poisoned wine, dress up fancy, lock the room, take the drink, then lie down on the bed and wait.

It explained most of the room. But Erin didn't like it. "Would she be able to lie still, like that, while the poison was taking effect?"

Levine considered. "I doubt it. Asphyxiation is painful. The victim usually convulses."

"So someone posed her," Erin said. "But maybe not the person who killed her. Someone could've found her already dead, arranged her..." She stopped. That was a pretty weird thought. Who would've done something like that, but not called the police? That made less sense than murder. She looked at Levine.

"Is this a suicide or a homicide?"

"Too early to make a diagnosis," the ME said. "If it's a poisoning, it depends how she was poisoned. It could also have been an accidental poisoning."

Erin sighed. "Okay, get her back to the lab. I know you've got the other two from this morning, but do what you can."

The CSU guys showed up as Levine was taking another look at the body. Erin pointed out what she had so far. They went to work with cameras, documenting the scene. Erin decided to head back to the precinct. She needed an ID on the victim. A young woman with two false identities seemed like a dead end, but she had an idea where to start.

*   *   *

The office of the head of the Precinct 8 Vice Squad was a converted maintenance closet. It was windowless, cheerless, and almost airless on account of an unreliable vent. Now that, Erin thought, was a room it'd be easy to gas someone in. When she and Rolf arrived in the doorway, Sergeant Brown, the Vice commander, was on the phone. His feet were propped on a desk covered with Chinese takeout boxes, candy wrappers, and sleazy magazines.

"Yeah, Monica, that sounds great," Brown said, holding up a finger to Erin. "Yeah, I'd love to see you in person. Fantastic. We'll make it a date. You wear that slinky red number you were talking about. Yeah, that one. I'll bring chocolates and you can eat 'em off my stomach. Yeah, like that, babe. You know that's what I like. Hey, honey, looking forward to it. You take care."

He hung up. "Sorry, O'Reilly. Work. You know how it is."

"Work," she repeated.

"Yeah. We got a 900 number we think is a front for a prostitution ring. We're trying to set up face-to-face meets with the girls, haul 'em in, maybe lean on 'em and grab some pimps." Brown sighed. "Y'know, when I first got put in Vice, I thought it'd be sexy. Guess I'd seen *Pretty Woman* too many times. I tell ya, nothing makes sex less sexy than working Vice. Now, I see a pretty girl, I just wanna have a normal conversation, y'know? About the weather, maybe, or the Yankees. Guess I oughta see a shrink. Anyway, what's up in the big leagues?"

"I've got a couple IDs I need you to run," she said, handing photocopies across the desk and being careful not to touch the layer of debris.

Brown dropped his feet to the floor, leaned forward with a squeak of the chair and another sigh, and took the papers. "Penelope Jackson, Jennifer Paxton," he said. "Huh. Different names, but they look like twins."

"Same girl," Erin said. "We pulled them off a Jane Doe in a hotel. I just need to know if Vice has anything under either of these aliases."

"She a hooker?"

"Could be. Nothing in the system for them, no arrests. We're waiting on prints."

Brown typed a query into his computer. "Okay, I got bubkis on Jackson. Paxton... huh. Got her listed as an associate of an escort service in central Manhattan. Don't know if that's her real name; we haven't brought her in for questioning yet. Guess we never will now. She's incidental. Her name got mentioned by a CI."

"What's the escort service called?" Erin asked.

"Classy Dames, Incorporated," Brown said. "I shit you not."

"Who thinks up these names?"

Brown shrugged. "Doesn't matter what they're called," he said. "Main question is, who thinks calling it an escort service is fooling anyone?"

"Damn," Erin said. "Last time I went after a prostitution ring, my car got shot full of holes."

Brown grinned. "Maybe next time you'll remember to use protection."

"You're an asshole, Brown," she said.

"So they tell me," he said. "I'll send you what we've got on these guys. Anything else?"

"Yeah," Erin said, turning for the door. "Give Monica my best."

*   *   *

Back in Major Crimes, she found the rest of the squad still going through shipping records. Vic was on the phone. The call didn't appear to be going well; he'd field-stripped his sidearm and was cleaning the weapon with savage efficiency while he kept the phone wedged on his shoulder.

"I'm on hold," he announced. "Port Authority. Seventeen minutes and counting."

"What's it look like, O'Reilly?" Webb asked.

"Can't say yet," she replied. "Levine's running a tox-screen. She thinks maybe cyanide poisoning."

"Murder, suicide, or accident?" he asked.

"Could be murder," she said. "But not an accident. The body was posed."

"How so?"

She described the scene. The others stopped their work to listen.

"Freaky," Jones said. "Maybe suicide. A little over thirty-five percent of female suicides are by hanging, but drugs are second most common, twenty-four point seven."

"I swear, you just make these numbers up," Vic said.

Jones gave him a look. "No, I just remember what I read. You know, reading? See, books have these little black marks on the pages. They're called letters, and together they make words..."

"And those words spell 'kiss my ass,'" Vic growled. He spun his chair around to face the wall and kept waiting on the phone.

"What's your gut say?" Webb asked Erin. "You think this was self-inflicted?"

Erin had been thinking about it. "Levine didn't want to make a ruling," she said. "The room wasn't disturbed. No signs of robbery or assault. The night lock was engaged. But..." she trailed off.

"It didn't feel right?"

She nodded.

"Well, we treat it like a homicide until we're sure," he said. "See what Levine can tell you. And run down this Classy Dames service. If the girl was targeted, one of her johns might've called them."

"What've we got on the two that washed up?" she asked.

"Not much. There's just too many ships. Anyone reports some missing crew, that'll be a start, but might not give us any answers. Sometimes guys jump ship when they hit port, just like in the old days. Can't wait to go on liberty."

"In the Royal Navy, they wouldn't pay their sailors when in port," Jones chimed in. "They thought it would increase desertion rates."

"As opposed to guys deserting because they hadn't been paid," Vic said over his shoulder.

"We're in a holding pattern for now," Webb said. "Neshenko's gonna liaise with Port Authority, get the word out, run pics of the victims to them. Maybe someone remembers something. Otherwise, we're waiting on lab work."

Erin sat down at her desk. She looked up Classy Dames, Incorporated, and got a phone number, along with a New Jersey address. "Great," she muttered.

"Problem?" Jones asked.

"I have to go to Jersey."

"I know a joke about that," Vic said. "You know why New Yorkers are depressed?"

"Why?"

"Because they know the light at the end of the tunnel is only New Jersey."

Webb snorted. "We don't need you here at the moment," he said to her. "You want to try them in person, go ahead."

Erin stood up again. "Come on, Rolf," she said. "Let's go talk to the escort service, which I'm sure is totally legitimate and absolutely not a front for prostitution."

"Careful, O'Reilly," Webb said. "You keep that cynical attitude, you'll end up just like me by the time you're forty."

"Don't even joke about that," she said.

*   *   *

Erin took the Lincoln Tunnel across the Hudson into Weehawken. Her GPS led her to an address that, whatever the name of the company, didn't look classy. It was a plain brick storefront in a generic strip mall. A small sign in the door identified Classy Dames, Inc., but that was it. Clearly, they did their business over the phone and Internet.

She scoped the place, looking for anything out of the ordinary. She'd been extra careful ever since the ambush that had nearly killed Vic on their last case. But nothing raised any red flags, so she parked, let Rolf out of his compartment, and headed in.

She entered a plain lobby, with the only furniture a wood-veneer desk from the Seventies, a computer and phone on the desk, and a chair behind it. A middle-aged woman sat in the chair, wearing too much makeup and a telephone headset. Erin looked around the room. No one else was there. No other chairs, no magazines, no brochures, not even a potted plant. It was just about the most depressing office she'd ever seen.

The woman glanced up at her. "You got an appointment?" she said in a thick, unpleasant Jersey accent. "Hey, no pets," she went on, without waiting for an answer.

"He's not a pet," Erin said, flashing her shield. "NYPD. I'd like to ask you some questions."

The phone rang. The woman held up her hand. "Hold onto your panties," she said and pushed a button on the phone. Her voice instantly changed, becoming a silky purr. "Hello there, sir."

Erin blinked. It didn't sound like the same woman. She was too startled to do anything for a moment.

"Why yes, I'd be delighted to. Have you patronized our service in the past? Yes, I see that. Why hello, Mr. Goodrich, yes, I thought I recognized your voice. Yes, Pamela is still in our employ. I'm so pleased you hear you say that. Yes, your satisfaction is our top priority."

Erin wanted to step outside and find a bush to throw up into. Her previous experience working prostitution cases had worn away whatever glamour it might have once had. She listened mechanically as the secretary set up an appointment, without ever actually mentioning sex. She could always claim Classy Dames just provided attractive arm candy for businessmen to take out to dinner, or to the theater, or whatever. Everyone knew what was really going on, but that wasn't the point. No wonder Sergeant Brown was so cynical.

Finally, the call ended. Erin stepped forward.

Before she could say anything, the secretary started talking. No more smooth bedroom voice. She was back to pure, no-nonsense Jersey. "Listen, honey, in case you haven't noticed, you crossed outta New York when you went over the river. So whatever you think you got on us, you better have a Jersey cop and a warrant with you, or you can take your questions and shove 'em."

Erin was used to this sort of thing. "I think you're misunderstanding me, ma'am," she said. "I don't have any interest in your business."

The woman looked a little surprised. "Then whatcha doin' here? Why don't you go back to the city so nice, they named it twice?"

"I need to talk to you about Jennifer Paxton," Erin said.

The secretary was unimpressed. "Should I know her?"

"You tell me," Erin said.

The other woman's face was totally blank.

Time to try a different tactic. "We think someone may have targeted her," she said.

"This Paxton chick, she in trouble?" the secretary asked, her tone making it clear she didn't much care one way or the other.

"Not anymore," Erin said.

"Then why you here?"

"She's dead."

"Whaddaya mean?" the woman said. It hadn't registered.

"What people usually mean," Erin said, giving it to her straight. "Not breathing. On a slab in the morgue. Dead."

"Oh," the secretary said, and her tough-girl front cracked. "Oh, shit."

"Yeah," Erin agreed. "So, you obviously knew her. You have a boss you think I should talk to?"

The secretary nodded. "Just a sec," she said and punched a button on her phone. "Mr. Lorimer? I've got a cop out front, says Jenny's... Jenny's dead." To Erin's surprise, it looked like the woman was having trouble getting the words out. She realized that Classy Dames wasn't being run by a street-corner pimp. In spite of the bland appearance of the office, this was a high-class call-girl operation. They weren't used to their girls getting killed. "No, we're not in trouble. Yeah, okay. I'll send her in."

The woman disconnected the call and pointed to the door in the back wall. "First one on the left," she said, then hesitated. "Was... was she... did someone...?"

"That's what we're trying to find out," Erin said. "Did Jenny have any family that you know about?"

The secretary shook her head. "I don't know. Jenny didn't talk about her home much. Ask Mr. Lorimer."

Erin went through the door, Rolf trotting beside her. The back rooms of the facility were more upscale. There were photos on the walls, mostly glamor shots of young women. On the left was an office, tastefully furnished, with a desk that looked to be real hardwood. A man in his forties, hair going a little gray at the edges, stood up and smiled at her.

"Good day, Officer," he said, extending his hand. "I'm Nate Lorimer." He had a nice smile, showing off a set of straight, white teeth. His suit was expensive without being flashy. Not a bad-looking guy. Erin reflected that pimps came in all shapes and sizes.

She kept her emotions under the surface and gave his hand a brief, firm shake. "Detective Erin O'Reilly, NYPD Major Crimes."

"Please, have a seat, Detective," he said. "Can I offer you anything to drink? Coffee, tea? What's your pleasure?"

"Coffee, please. Cream, no sugar." He had a pot right there in his office, and she could smell it. It was an expensive brew, a lot better than the sludge that came out of the machine at the precinct.

He poured her a cup, and took one for himself. Once they were settled in their chairs, he said, "What can I do for you, Detective?"

"Do you have a Jennifer Paxton working for your company?" she asked, going straight in.

"Yes," he said. "Or, perhaps I should say, I did. Norma told me over the phone that something has happened to Miss Paxton."

"She was found dead in a hotel room in Manhattan this morning," Erin said. "I'm investigating."

Lorimer's face gave nothing away. He merely looked politely distressed by the news. "I'm very sorry to hear that," he said. "Jenny is... was... a lovely young woman. Outgoing, vivacious, one of our most popular girls. Any client who hired her was bound to ask for her again. I do hope nothing... untoward occurred. Since the police are involved, am I wrong to assume there is some concern regarding possible foul play?"

"We're still determining that," Erin said. "And you can help us narrow down the possibilities. What can you tell me about Jenny?"

Lorimer rubbed his upper lip with one hand. "Well, for starters, her name is not Jennifer Paxton," he said.

Erin wasn't surprised. Hookers and actors were fond of stage names. "Do you know her real name?"

"Janice Barnes," Lorimer said.

"Do you have family contact information?"

He shook his head. "I'm afraid not. We do run background checks on our employees, of course. This is a high-class establishment. Our clients expect a well-educated young woman who is an accomplished conversationalist, able to function in the circles of high society. A college degree is appreciated."

Erin held up a hand. "Mr. Lorimer, I'm well aware of your business," she said. "I'm not investigating Classy Dames, Incorporated. I'm just trying to find out who might have wanted to harm Miss Barnes. Was she working last night?"

"One moment," Lorimer said, tapping the keys on his computer. "Yes, she had an appointment last night."

Erin's heart leaped. "You have a name?"

"John Anderson," he said dryly.

"So, not a real name."

"Probably not. It's hardly unheard-of in this business."

"Do you have a recording of his call?"

"He made the request through our website," Lorimer said. "Shy customers aren't exactly uncommon. The appointment was for eight o'clock."

"Where?"

"She was to go to Shakespeare Garden in Central Park," he said. "Wearing a black dress and carrying a rose."

"That strike you as a little weird?" Erin asked.

Lorimer gave her a look. "Detective, in my line of work, that doesn't even come close to weird."

"Right," Erin said, sorry she'd asked. "How'd he pay?"

"In advance, by credit card," Lorimer said. "We require it. It's a confidential service, of course."

"I'll need that credit card info," Erin said.

"And I'll be happy to provide it," Lorimer said. "As soon as I see a court order." He smiled apologetically. "Confidential, as I said. We value our reputation for discretion."

"Anything else you can tell me?"

"I'm afraid not."

She stood up and gave him one of her cards. "If you think of anything, please give me a call," she said. "I think Miss Barnes might've been murdered. If that's the case, then the rest of your girls may be in danger, too."

"I'm surprised you care, Detective," Lorimer said. "Most in your profession don't."

Erin paused in the doorway. "Mr. Lorimer," she said, "I don't care what a murder victim did for a living, unless it tells me something that helps crack the case. I don't give a damn if she was a hooker, a stripper, or a nun. I'll still catch the son of a bitch who did it. Hell," she finished, "I'd even take down someone who clipped you."

Chapter 4

Erin called Webb from her car, explaining what she'd found out from Lorimer. "I didn't get a lot," she finished. "I'll need a court order for the credit card."

"It'll be stolen, of course," Webb said. "At the end of the month, some poor bastard's gonna have some explaining to do when his wife sees his bill."

"What do you want me to do?" she asked.

"Come on back. Regroup."

"Roger that."

Erin spent the rest of the day at the precinct, running down what she could on Janice Barnes. She didn't get much. Apparently Janice had moved to Jersey from Georgia. She'd had a few brushes with the law, but nothing serious. No felonies, no prostitution charges.

It was depressing. The rest of the squad were feeling it, too. They were getting nowhere on the two gunshot victims. Vic hunched over his desk growling. Jones stared blankly at her computer screen, which hadn't changed in half an hour. And Webb spent his time muttering darkly about how much he missed Los Angeles and his time in the LAPD. It was a relief when the clock hit five.

Erin stood up. "Guess I'll call it," she said.

"We'll shake this again tomorrow," Jones said. "See what comes loose. Hey Erin, you want to go somewhere, catch a bite?"

Erin wasn't in the mood for police company. "Rain check," she said.

"Have it your way," Jones replied. "Don't drink yourself into a stupor, okay?"

"Why not?" she tossed over her shoulder on the way to the stairs. "I'm Irish, aren't I?"

It wasn't a completely terrible idea. She wanted a drink, bad. She drove home first, walked Rolf, and gave him his supper. Then she considered the places near her apartment and walked to the closest joint.

She had a history with the Barley Corner. Its proprietor, Morton Carlyle, was the canniest, most polite member of the Irish Mob in New York City. He'd known her father back when Sean O'Reilly had worked Patrol, and Erin had renewed the family's relationship earlier that year. Carlyle had been a suspect in a murder investigation, but he'd been cleared in the end. The real perp had tried to blow up Carlyle's pub, and through quick thinking and dumb luck, she'd managed to save the building. She'd also saved the lives of Carlyle, his best mate Corky, and a few others into the bargain. That meant, in Carlyle's book, that he owed her a favor, and that her money was no good at his bar.

A free drink sounded awfully nice, so that was where she went. The Corner was always busy in the evenings, full of a crowd of mostly Irishmen, about half of them mob-connected. But even though they knew Erin was with the NYPD, or maybe because of it, they always made her feel welcome.

She saw Carlyle right away, impeccably dressed, hair shining silver in the overhead lights. He was at his place of honor at the bar, arms resting on it, facing the room. He was watching a European soccer game on the big-screen TV. Erin knew he ran a sports book under the counter out of the bar. She might even be able to prove it, but what would be the point? He'd been a valuable resource in solving her last case, and underworld contacts were useful to a detective. Better to keep him where he was, and to stay on good terms with him.

One man she didn't see in the place was Corky Corcoran. That was just as well. He'd been trying to charm her into bed with him ever since they'd met, and that was a headache she didn't need tonight. Erin went to the bar and flagged down the bartender.

"Hey, Danny," she said.

"Evening, Erin," he said with a grin. He was one of the guys she'd helped save from getting blown to pieces, so he had a soft spot for her. "What can I get you?"

"Double scotch," she said. "House brand."

"Straight up?"

"On the rocks." The day had gotten hot and the air conditioning in the precinct hadn't been able to keep up.

He set the glass on the counter, dropped the ice cubes into it, and poured a double of Glen D whiskey. The ice cracked as the liquor cascaded over it. Erin took the glass, found a spot at the bar, and took a sip. It burned and chilled at the same time. She took a second to let the whiskey dissipate on her tongue. She felt it all the way through her nose and the roof of her mouth. It burned some of the fog out of her brain. She took another drink.

"Erin, darling, it's a fine thing to be seeing you this evening."

She turned at the distinctive Irish brogue. "Evening, Cars," she said to Carlyle. It was a nickname he'd picked up in his home country. It was an open secret that, before coming to America, he'd built car bombs for the IRA. Erin still couldn't believe she was on speaking terms with a retired terrorist, but in spite of his past, she actually liked him.

Carlyle gestured to the stool next to her, which had opened up as if by magic. "May I?"

"It's your bar."

"Thank you," he said, taking the seat. "And how go your efforts to bring law and order to our fair city?"

She snorted. "Shitty."

"Are you wanting to talk about it?"

"To *you*?"

"And why not? I've some insight into the world we both inhabit."

Erin shook her head. "You're a piece of work," she said. "We can't give details of ongoing investigations. You know that."

"I'm wounded, Erin," he said, giving her a pained expression. "I'm terribly afraid you're confusing me with a member of the press. I'm a respectable gangster, remember? We may do any number of things, but we don't go spreading information to the general public."

"Respectable gangster," she repeated. But she couldn't deny he was right. Carlyle was a lot of things, but he wasn't indiscreet. All the same, she had to be careful what she told him. "I'm working an apparent suicide," she said.

"As a Major Crimes detective?"

"We've got to treat them as homicides until we know for sure," she explained. "Even if they look like suicide."

"Your careful use of the word 'apparent' suggests you think otherwise."

She hesitated, then nodded. "Yeah. It feels weird. Too many little details out of place."

Carlyle raised two fingers to Danny, then pointed to Erin's drink. Danny brought two more whiskeys, one for each of them.

Carlyle curled his fingers around his glass, watching Erin. "Was it staged to resemble a suicide, then?" he asked quietly.

She thought it over. "No," she said finally. "Not staged... it was posed."

"As what?" he asked. "To implicate someone else, perhaps? Or to take the appearance of an accident?"

"No," she said again. "She was posed on the bed, wearing a nice dress, fresh flowers in her hands. Makeup on her face."

"How did your victim perish, may I ask?"

"Poison. She drank it, we think. Still waiting on the final lab work."

"That certainly sounds like suicide," Carlyle said. "Unless she was forced to drink it, or took it unawares, in which case it's exceedingly unlikely you'd have found her so composed."

"Which would mean the killer was in the room after she was dead," Erin said. "Yeah, I thought of that. Problem is, the room was locked. From the inside."

"Hotel?" he asked.

"Yeah."

"Upper floor?"

"Of course." She smiled sourly. "The windows don't even open, so no one could get in or out that way."

"Was it a deadbolt, or a chain lock?"

"What's the difference?" Erin said. "It was a chain, but those can't be jimmied easily from outside. Not without leaving marks."

Carlyle shrugged. "It's not so difficult. I know a lad. In his younger and more foolish days, he'd a habit of entering hotel rooms and taking things which didn't belong to him."

"How'd he do it?" Erin asked.

"He took a job with the hotel as a cleaner," Carlyle explained. "He acquired access to the hotel's keycard program.

Then he simply let himself into the relevant rooms and adjusted the chain locks."

"Adjusted how?"

"He replaced the chain with a slightly longer one," he said with a smile. "At a glance, the chain would appear no different, but this lad was slightly built and could ease his hand through the gap."

"So he could unlock it from outside, and even lock it again when he was done," Erin said, getting it. "Shit. We didn't even think to measure the chain. But what about the keycards? I thought those were only good for a day or two."

"They are," Carlyle said. "From my understanding, your lad would need access to the hotel's computers, in order to program his own card."

Erin's mind was racing. "So he's probably an employee."

"That follows," Carlyle said. "But are you certain you're not pursuing a ghost? Your unfortunate victim may have drunk poison, wiped her mouth, lain down, and quietly perished."

Wiped her mouth, Erin thought. Then she made a double connection. "No way," she said. "Her lipstick was fresh. It wasn't even smudged. It was put on after she'd drunk." She looked at Carlyle with a triumphant smile. "And I saw her cosmetic kit in the bathroom. Her lipstick was there, but it was the wrong goddamn color. It's murder, all right." She slid off her stool.

He returned the smile. "I'm glad to be of assistance, Erin. But you've not finished your drink. Sit down again, if you please. There's many sins an Irishman can commit, and may yet be forgiven, but wasting good whiskey is unpardonable."

Erin laughed and returned to her seat. "I'll do that," she said. She was feeling a lot better.

"Then I'll drink with you," he said, raising his glass. "To your success. Have you any idea why your lass might have been murdered?"

"I don't know. It's possible she was dead before the perp was even in the room. But he took the time to lay her out, dress her up, put on makeup... Christ, he brought her a bouquet. The roses weren't even wilted when I saw the scene. It was creepy. It was like he wanted to see her dead, but still looking her best."

"You're saying it's a man who did this?" Carlyle inquired. "May I ask why?"

She looked him straight in the eye. "Because nine times out of ten, serial killers are men."

Chapter 5

Carlyle didn't say anything. He rubbed his chin and watched her thoughtfully. Erin drained the last of her double whiskey. The ice cubes clinked as she set the glass down on the bar. She stood up.

"I've gotta go," she said.

"Of course you do," he said, rising politely. "Thank you for stopping in. As always, it's a pleasure. I hope I've been some small assistance."

Her phone buzzed. "Yeah, thanks," she said as she reached for it. She wasn't surprised to see Webb's name on the caller ID. She'd been about to call him anyway. "Catch you later, Carlyle."

She put the phone to her ear on her way out the door. "Sir," she said. "I've got something on the hotel case."

"Is it an emergency?"

"No, but—" she began.

"Save it," Webb said. "We're going to Pier 16. Meet us there."

"But sir," she said. "This is important."

"So's this," Webb snapped. "Tell me about it later. We've got the boat from the shootings, and we need your K-9. It's gonna be a late night." He hung up.

Erin stared at her phone, feeling a little sick to her stomach. Her good mood had evaporated instantly. It wasn't a big deal, she told herself. He was just preoccupied with the other case. But she had to fight the sudden urge to throw her phone on the pavement. She went home instead, to fetch her car and her dog. It was time to go back to work. She just wished she'd stopped at the first glass of Scotch.

*   *   *

The sun was going down by the time she got to the dock. Jones met Erin and Rolf at the parking lot at the base of the pier. Jones had obviously been dragged back in without much notice. She was dressed for a night on the town: tall boots, a miniskirt, and a halter top. She'd hung her shield on a chain around her neck, where it nestled amid a jumble of charms and necklaces.

"Hot date?" Erin asked, raising her eyebrows.

Jones rolled her eyes. "I thought maybe I'd get lucky tonight, but I hadn't even gotten started. Come on, I'll take you to the ship. The others are already on board."

"What've we got?" Erin asked.

"We heard from the Port Authority," Jones explained as they walked. "A boat got flagged with a couple of crew missing. Skipper claimed they'd jumped ship before going through customs."

"Can they do that?" Erin asked.

"Not legally," Jones said. "Homeland Security gets pissed about it, but what can you do? The only reason this one came to us is because we asked specifically about two missing guys."

"What's the ship?" Erin asked. They were coming up on it now, a rust-spotted old tramp steamer.

"The *Loch Druich*, out of Glasgow," Jones said.

"I'm not gonna have to spell that in my reports, am I?"

Jones laughed. "I've got it written down."

On the deck, they found Webb and Vic talking to a rough-looking man who looked to be in his mid-fifties. It was a warm night, but he was wearing a thick woolen sweater and watch cap. He was edgy. His hands kept creeping toward his pockets, but every time they did, Vic cleared his throat and the guy dropped them again. Police didn't like interviewees' hands where they couldn't see them.

Webb glanced at the two women. "O'Reilly, glad to see you," he said. "This is Captain MacIntosh. The captain was just explaining to me how we don't need to look around, because we won't find anything."

"Tha's right," MacIntosh said with a thick Scottish burr in his voice. "I dinnae know what ye think ye're looking for, but there's nae lad aboard to be found, and nae sign of them. I tell ye, they've buggered off."

"Then you won't mind us taking a look," Vic said, in a tone that suggested he didn't care whether the captain minded or not.

"Och, as ye will," the captain said. Then he caught sight of Rolf and blinked. "What is that beastie doing aboard?"

"Taking a look," Erin said. Then, to Webb, "Do we have anything belonging to the victims?"

Vic smiled grimly and produced a pair of paper bags. Each one contained a sock. He'd come prepared.

"Okay," she said. "Let's do this."

Vic knelt in front of Rolf and opened the bags, being careful not to touch the contents.

"Rolf, *such*," Erin said, giving him his search command.

The German Shepherd sniffed carefully, then planted his nose on the deck and was off.

It wouldn't hold up in court, but Erin was very quickly convinced that the victims had been on this ship. Rolf crisscrossed the deck, side to side, to and from the door to the bridge. It would've looked aimless to an untrained observer, but Erin knew he was following the paths the men had taken. Unfortunately, they'd been all over the ship, and the dog didn't know which trail to follow. But he was particularly interested in a straight line from the hatch to the stern rail.

Vic walked alongside them, staring at the deck. The pier was floodlit, but the ship had patches of shadow, and he played a big D-cell flashlight along their path. He had an evidence kit in his other hand, in case they found anything. "I think we might have blood here," he said, pointing to a dark brown smear. "Hard to tell with all the rust."

"Mark it for the CSU guys," she said. "You think this is where they bought it?"

He shrugged. "Maybe. Or someone did 'em in the hold, then dragged 'em and dumped 'em over the side."

"Let's check inside," she said. "The captain said it was okay, so we're clear, right?"

"The LT's got a warrant," Vic said. "We can go anywhere."

The corridors of the *Loch Druich* were in lousy shape. Pipes were leaky and corroded. Something green seemed to be growing on the lower panels of the bulkheads, and there was a smell Erin couldn't identify which reminded her of a locker room that hadn't been cleaned in a while. Rolf made a beeline straight for a steep stairway. They followed it down. The only light belowdecks was Vic's flashlight.

"Hope we didn't pull you off a big night," Erin said, trying to take her mind off their surroundings. The place was giving her the creeps.

Vic snorted but didn't say anything.

"You doing okay with... everything?" she asked awkwardly. They still hadn't talked about the shooting they'd been involved in.

"Why wouldn't I be?" he retorted.

She didn't have an answer for that, even though she guessed it was bullshit, so it was almost a relief when she caught a glimpse of a smear of rusty brown on the wall. "Hold it! Pan right, where you just were."

He saw it too. "That's blood. This is it."

Rolf went to the end of the corridor and whined at the closed hatch. Erin donned her gloves and turned the circular handle in the middle of the door, swinging it open.

The smell of blood wasn't strong, and almost got lost in the greasy, mechanical odors of the engine room, but to Rolf it might as well have been the only scent in the world. He homed in and went to the middle of the room. There wasn't much space. The steamer's engine took up most of the area. Vic, intent on the ground, bashed his head on a low-hanging pipe. He cursed and rubbed his forehead.

"What the hell," he muttered. "There's nothing here. Maybe if CSU can match the blood, we've got something, but it'll take weeks to get the DNA back from the lab."

Erin nodded. She flicked the light switch, hoping to get a better look. It didn't help much. There was a single dim bulb in the ceiling. It made an obnoxious buzzing sound when she turned it on, as if a fly was caught inside.

Then Rolf shoved his snout underneath part of the machinery. He took deep, heavy sniffs and whined again.

"What's he after?" Vic wondered aloud. "We've got the bodies already. There somebody else stuffed under there?"

Erin, trying not to think about the condition of the floor, dropped to her belly and laid her head alongside her dog's.

"Hand me the light," she said. Vic passed it to her. She shone it into the space. The beam reflected off something small, about the size of a dime, that was white and red.

"Got something here," she said. "You got tweezers?"

Vic opened his evidence kit and handed down the forceps. Erin eased her hand into the space. Even with her small frame, her arm barely fit. She carefully took the small thing between the tips of the forceps and slowly drew it out.

"Looks like a guitar pick," Vic observed.

"Yeah," Erin said. "I think it's a fingernail."

"Damn," Vic said. "I'm never gonna look at a musician the same way again."

"I don't know if they were killed here," she said. "But I'll bet this is where they were tortured."

"What for?" he wondered.

She shrugged. "How the hell do I know?" She got a baggie from Vic's kit and bagged the nail. "We gotta get CSU in here, do the whole room."

"Let's go tell the boss," Vic said.

*   *   *

Webb was so happy with their news that he actually smiled. The first thing he said was, "Good work." The next thing out of his mouth was, "Captain MacIntosh, you're going to need to come in to the station with us."

"Why?" the captain demanded. "I dinnae do anything."

"Just to answer some questions," Webb said.

"Am I under arrest?"

"Of course not," Webb said.

"Then I will nae come with you."

"In that case," Webb said, "you're under arrest. Neshenko?"

Vic produced his cuffs.

"Och," MacIntosh said. "Ye're a bloody great bloke, aren't ye? Nae need for the bracelets, I'll come quietly. But I'm a Scottish citizen."

"And the victims died in American waters," Jones said. "We have jurisdiction."

"I demand to speak to my consul," MacIntosh said.

"You'll have your phone call," Webb sighed.

"I hate when it gets political," Vic muttered.

"Jones," Webb said. "Call some uniforms and secure the ship. Get CSU to go over the whole thing, stem to stern. Once they're here, you and O'Reilly come back to the precinct. Neshenko, you're escorting Captain MacIntosh with me."

"I was kinda thinking I'd go home," Vic said.

"Am I interrupting your evening, Detective?"

"Yes, sir, you are."

"Were you planning a busy night of staring at your TV and drinking vodka straight from the bottle?" the Lieutenant asked.

"Something like that."

"You'll have time for that later. We need to talk to the captain here."

"Och, dinnae trouble yourself on my account," the captain said.

*   *   *

While they waited for the uniforms and the evidence techs, Jones filled Erin in on what they knew about the ship.

"She's Scottish registered, home port of Glasgow," she explained. "Sailed with five crew, including the captain. Cargo of woolen clothes and a few cases of whiskey. It's a brand I haven't heard of. Glen something-or-other." Jones glanced at her notebook. "Docherty-Kinlochewe. I have no idea if I'm saying that right."

"Glen D?" Erin said, sparked with sudden interest.

"You know it?" Jones asked, surprised.

"Hell," Erin said. "I had some right before I came down here."

"How is it?"

"It's the good stuff."

"Anyway," Jones said, "Captain MacIntosh and two of the crew sailed in. Reginald McCandless and Simon Wright. The other two, Sean Garrity and Daniel Carr, weren't on board."

"So they're our victims?"

"Probably. The Lieutenant's going to have MacIntosh take a look at the bodies, see if he'll ID them."

"What if he doesn't?" Erin said. "I didn't get the feeling he wanted to help us solve this one."

"Then we tie them to the boat with the physical evidence," Jones said. "The evidence you and your boy got us." She nodded to Rolf, who gave her a brief, disinterested look and went back to his Kong chew-toy. Erin had given it to him as a reward for finding the fingernail, and Rolf was enjoying his wages. "Then we threaten to charge him as an accessory," Jones went on, "and see if he cracks. Hell, for all we know, he did it himself."

"Think CSU will find the gun on board?" Erin asked.

Jones shrugged. "Not if the shooter was smart. If he knew what he was doing, he ditched it overboard along with the bodies and it's somewhere in the Atlantic."

"If he was really smart, he'd have weighted the corpses down with something, so they didn't float ashore," Erin said.

The first wave of Patrol officers arrived to secure the scene. The two detectives were kept busy directing traffic until the CSU van arrived and the techs started working over the ship. Then they left for the precinct. It was after nine o'clock by the time they pulled into the garage, and the night's end was nowhere in sight.

*　　*　　*

"He lawyer up yet?" Jones asked as they walked into Major Crimes.

"Nah," Vic said. "We've got him in Room One, softening up." The big Russian snorted. "He's gonna crack."

"How you figure?" Erin asked.

"We took him down to the morgue, showed him the stiffs," Vic said. "He just about painted the floor with his lunch. He's no hard case."

"He's also not our guy," Webb said. "But maybe he knows who is."

"You sure about that, sir?" Jones asked.

"Sure as I can be," he said. "The only reason he hasn't already talked is that he's scared of someone else. I'm guessing that's the killer."

"Sir," Erin said.

"Right," Webb said. "You've got something on our other case. So, homicide or suicide?"

"I think it's worse than that."

Webb's eyes narrowed. "What do you mean?"

"The guy who did this," she said. "I think it's part of a series."

There were a couple of seconds of complete silence. Even Vic was staring at her in astonishment.

"I don't think I heard you right," Webb said.

Erin was nettled. He'd heard her perfectly damn well. "It's got planning. Careful execution. He set it up ahead of time, fixed the lock so he could get in, then lock it again on the way out. He poisoned her, then posed her all dressed up. This guy gets a thrill out of it. I'm sure of it."

"What are you now, an FBI profiler?" Webb demanded.

She was startled at his tone. "No, I just think it fits the way a serial—" she began, stumbling a little over her thoughts.

"No," Webb snapped, cutting her off. He advanced on her, backing her up to the wall of the office. He put his finger right in her face. "Don't say that word again, not in here, and sure as hell not on the street."

"Why not?" she shot back. She was feeling defensive, and that always made her angry. He had her pinned against the wall, so she felt trapped, too, even though he hadn't touched her. She reflexively braced for a physical confrontation.

"Listen to me, O'Reilly," Webb said in a low voice, biting off his words one by one. "Listen very carefully. We have hundreds of murders every year in this city. One in a hundred, *maybe*, is part of a series. And what happens when someone hears that word? Press. You want reporters hanging around you every step of the way, talking to your witnesses and suspects, digging into your family, nosing into everything? You think you can do your job that way?"

"That isn't the point," she said.

"That's exactly the point," Webb said. "Even if you're right, *if*, it's not going to help you catch the guy if you start sounding off about him being the next Bundy or Gacy. And here's the thing, O'Reilly. You've got good instincts. You're good police. You're shaping up to be a fine detective. But you're still new at this. You don't have the training, or the experience, to make a call like this. Besides, you're still shook up from the Russian thing."

That was a low blow. Erin couldn't believe he'd bring up the shooting incident as a point against her. "I'm fine!" she snapped.

"Are you?" he challenged. "You going to tell me you sleep just fine, no nightmares, no flashbacks?"

"You've read my psych evaluation?" she blurted out. "Those are confidential!"

"Of course I haven't," Webb said, and she saw she'd fallen for a classic interrogator's trick. She'd forgotten how good he was at getting people to admit things. But he didn't look smug. He mostly just looked tired. "Look," he said. "This job takes a toll on us. Forget about the case for tonight. Go home, get some rest if you can. I'm sorry I had to drag you in here."

"I'm fine," she said again. "I don't need special treatment."

Jones put a hand on Erin's shoulder. "Erin," she said gently. "Maybe you should listen to the Lieutenant. He's—"

Erin shook the hand off. "Dammit, I'm fine!" She looked across the room at Vic, who was watching the argument in silence. "He went through the same shit I did, and you're not sending him home. If this is because I'm a woman..."

"That's got nothing to do with it," Webb said, and Erin got a little satisfaction out of the defensive tone that had crept into his own voice. "Neither one of you is going to be in that interrogation room. Jones and I will conduct. If you insist on being present, you can observe next door. We clear?"

Erin swallowed all the things she wanted to say and nodded, her jaw clenched tight.

"Good," Webb said. He took a deep breath. "And again, excellent work finding that fingernail. That ties the victims to the ship. That's how we build cases. Evidence, not speculation."

She gritted her teeth and nodded again.

Chapter 6

Webb and Jones sat down opposite Captain MacIntosh in the interrogation room. The Scotsman looked nervously from one of them to the other. Webb folded his hands on the table and stared at the other man without speaking.

Vic, watching with Erin through the one-way observation mirror, nodded and smiled in a mean-spirited way.

"What?" Erin demanded. She was still pissed off.

"Wouldn't work on a tough guy, someone who's been through the system," he said. "But this boy's a civilian."

Erin looked back into the interrogation room. Nothing was happening. Jones was studying her fingernails, leaning casually back in her chair. Webb was still watching MacIntosh, who was getting more and more fidgety.

"Break 'em with silence," Vic explained. "The other guy talks first, the Lieutenant's halfway home."

"All right," MacIntosh burst out. "What are ye waiting for?"

Webb raised his eyebrows in mild surprise. "Me? I'm waiting for my guy with Homeland Security to get here."

"What's that to do with me?" MacIntosh asked. "I'm nae terrorist!"

Webb blinked. Jones sat forward and gave the other man her full attention.

"I didn't mention terrorism," Webb said quietly. "But if that's something you're involved in, I'm sure they'll sort it out. That's above my pay grade. Of course, they'll want to be questioning you at their own facility, and in their own time."

"What are ye talking about?" the captain asked. He was starting to sweat.

"They keep talking about shutting down Guantanamo Bay," Webb said. "But I don't think they've gotten around to it yet."

"I'm not even an American!" protested MacIntosh.

"Makes it easier," Webb said. "They'll probably classify you as an enemy combatant, until they can figure out exactly who you're working for, and why. Doesn't even have to go through our courts. Then? Who knows?"

"For the love of God, I've done nothing!" MacIntosh cried out. "What is it ye want from me?"

"When I took you in, I just wanted to ask about Garrity and Carr," Webb said. "Find out who killed them, catch a murderer. But that was before we checked the shipping manifest."

Erin shot Vic a quizzical look. He shrugged.

"Beats me," he muttered. "Kira was looking through 'em. She must've found something."

"All my papers are in perfect order!" MacIntosh said.

Jones laid a piece of paper on the table. An item was circled in red ink. "Except for one discrepancy, Captain," she said. "Can you explain why your manifest lists twelve cases of Glen Docherty-Kinlochewe whiskey, but only ten cases were in your hold?"

"It's pronounced Docherty-Kinlochewe," MacIntosh said.

Jones blinked. "That's what I said."

"Nae, lass, ye said Docherty-Kinlochewe."

There was an awkward silence.

Webb shrugged it away. "Whatever," he said. "The point is, there's two missing cases of Scotch."

"Whiskey goes missing around Scotsmen. Is that a federal offense?" MacIntosh demanded.

"That depends," Jones said. "There's some debate regarding whether maritime terrorism constitutes acts of piracy."

The only words MacIntosh heard were "terrorism" and "piracy." He looked wildly around the room. Erin thought he might be about to throw up or even faint.

"For God's sake," the poor guy whispered. "I did nae even know what was in the boxes."

"Bingo," Vic said softly.

"I know it wasn't whiskey," Webb said, leaning forward. "Two men don't get tortured and murdered over a few bottles of Scotch. What was in those boxes, Captain?"

"I dinnae know!" MacIntosh said. "You have tae believe me! I dinnae ask any questions, I just carry the cargo! Sean and Danny were looking after it!"

"Smuggling," Erin said to Vic. "How'd she know to check the manifest?"

He shrugged. "Kira checks details. And she remembers them."

"Captain," Webb said in a quiet, encouraging voice. "I know you didn't kill these guys. And I know the man who killed them took two cases marked Glen... Glen whatever. Now, Homeland Security doesn't give a damn whether you're involved or not. As far as they know, these cases were full of bombs, or nerve gas, or guns. They're going to be worried about what's going to happen to that cargo. Now, I don't know if it's weapons in those missing cases, but I won't be the one asking those questions anyway. All I care about is solving these murders. I can't protect you if you don't help me. If you don't know anything about it, then there's no way I can justify keeping you here, under New York Police protection. But if you can help me, then I can tell the Feds you're a cooperative witness, and we can keep you safe here with us while this whole thing gets laid to rest."

MacIntosh hesitated. "You'll protect me? From your government? And from *him*?"

Webb didn't ask who *he* was. He just nodded. "You have my word."

"Very well," MacIntosh said. "I dinnae know much, but what I know, I'll tell you."

Erin turned to Vic. "Did he just get this guy to ask us to keep him under arrest?"

"Yeah," Vic said. "Beautiful, isn't it? Sometimes I want to kiss the Lieutenant. Then I look at him, and the urge goes away, but it's there for a second or two."

"Danny and Sean worked for a lad in Glasgow," MacIntosh was saying. "I dinnae know his full name, but he's called Smiling Jack. He represents a band of hard men who specialize in moving things from place to place."

"This Smiling Jack," Webb said. "What can you tell me about him?"

"He's nae cheerful nor pleasant," the captain said. "I'm guessing he got the name on account of his grin."

"Glasgow smile," Vic said.

Erin wasn't familiar with the term, and told him so.

"Street thug punishment over there," he explained. "Use a knife or a straight razor, lay open the cheeks on both sides, extend the mouth."

"Right," Erin said, swallowing.

"He deals in cash," MacIntosh went on. "Nae questions asked. You dinnae argue with Smiling Jack. I carry Glen Docherty-Kinlochewe all the time, and usually it's just the whiskey, aye?"

"How do you know it's only whiskey?" Jones asked.

"Nae men come along with the shipments," MacIntosh said. "They only come on special voyages."

"How frequently?" Webb asked.

"Perhaps three, four times a year."

"You ever open any of these boxes?"

"Nae," the captain said, looking shocked. Then he paused. "But they're heavy, and well-packed. And they've a smell about them."

"What kind of smell?" Webb asked.

"Sometimes a smell of machine oil," he replied. "Sometimes a sort of putty smell, like modeler's clay."

"Like clay," Webb repeated.

Erin had taken some basic demolition training when she'd worked with Rolf on explosive detection. She yanked out her phone and tapped out a quick text to Webb, just two letters. The Lieutenant's hand went to his pocket when he felt the buzz. He glanced at the screen, nodded once, and put his phone back.

"What'd you send?" Vic asked.

"C4," Erin said.

Vic's eyes widened. "Plastic explosive? You sure?"

"Well," she said, "they could be smuggling plasticine instead."

"Christ," Vic said. "Gunrunners. I didn't know your nose was trained to ID chemicals."

"Not many of them," she said. "But my K-9 instructor was a little wacky. He thought we ought to know what our dogs were smelling, so he kept making us shove our noses in the same stuff they were training on."

"You don't even need the dog," he said. "We should just put a leash around your neck."

"You just try it. But it's useful, knowing smells." She paused. A thought was chasing her. "Smells," she said again. "Fragrances."

"I don't follow."

"The perfume," Erin said, snapping her fingers. "Do we know the fragrance? From the hotel?"

"How the hell would I know?" Vic retorted. "It's your case. You didn't tell me shit about it."

"The hotel room with my victim was full of perfume," she explained. "If we can find out what it is, maybe we can trace a sale."

"Yeah, great, do that," he said, turning back to the observation window. "But do it tomorrow. We're missing stuff here."

Erin started paying attention again. MacIntosh was talking about what had happened to the boxes.

"This bloody motor launch came alongside us, just after two in the morning," he said. "I dinnae know about it until they were aboard. Three lads, great big ones, carrying guns. They were wearing masks. They knew exactly what they were looking for. Poor Danny and Sean were asleep, thinking we were still well out to sea. They never had a chance.

"The leader of these pirates took them below with one of his lads, into the engine room," MacIntosh went on. "The other lad held his piece on myself and the rest of the crew. The engines were loud, but we could still hear the screaming."

The captain gulped and wiped his forehead. "Horrible, it was. It went on for half an hour, maybe a bit longer. Then we heard two gunshots, and they dragged the poor lads topside and dumped them over the rail. I thought we were next. After that, two of them went below again, and came up with a case each of the Docherty-Kinlochewe. They hoisted them down to a couple of other lads in their own boat. Then the leader said he'd be seeing us again, if we blabbed any of it to any man, and they left."

"So you heard his voice," Webb said. "What did he sound like?"

"A foreign chap," MacIntosh said.

Webb sighed. "From which country?"

"Germany, I'm thinking," MacIntosh said. "Or some such place."

Webb stood up. "I'll need you to write out a statement, Captain MacIntosh," he said. "Don't leave anything out. Take your time. Detective Jones will assist. There's some things I need to take care of."

* * *

Vic and Erin met Webb outside the interrogation room. "C4?" Webb snapped at Erin. "How sure are you?"

"I didn't smell it myself," she said. "But that's something that smells a little like modeling clay, and might be smuggled."

"Fantastic," Webb said. "Which is worse? Military-grade explosives being smuggled into New York, or those explosives getting ripped off by other criminals?"

"What do you want us to do?" Erin asked. "Won't we hand this off to Homeland Security when they get here?"

"O'Reilly," Webb said patiently, "Homeland Security's not coming. I made that up."

"Oh," she said, feeling foolish. "Right."

"But I'll need to report it to them now," he said. "So for tonight, go home and get some sleep, both of you. Keep working your cases. I'll let you know."

Chapter 7

Erin snapped awake, smelling gunpowder and blood, seeing flashing red-and-blue police lights. She grabbed for her gun in her nightstand, then stopped. Her bedroom was dark and quiet. There was no sign of danger.

She turned on the bedside lamp and ran a hand through her hair. Rolf lifted his head and blinked sleepily at her.

"It's okay, boy," she told him. "Go back to sleep."

Rolf didn't know that command, but he curled his snout behind his tail and closed his eyes again.

Erin lay back on her pillow and stared at the ceiling. Her heart was still pounding. Adrenaline drove away all thoughts of sleep. As she tried to let her pulse slow down, she glanced at the clock. It read 3:33.

"Shit," she said.

Her shootouts with the Russians were what the police called "Critical Incidents." She'd been required to see the NYPD psych guy, Doc Evans, to unpack what had happened. But Erin didn't want to talk about it. She just wanted to get back to work and put that case in her rearview mirror.

The shrink wasn't buying it. Didn't she feel some regret or remorse? She'd never killed anyone before.

No, she didn't feel any remorse. The bastard she'd shot had been an evil man who'd done terrible things to innocent young women. Plus, he'd been trying to kill her. There wasn't anything to regret. If she wasn't supposed to put him down, why had the NYPD issued her a gun in the first place?

But if that was all true, why did she keep waking up in the middle of the night? Why did she have to keep reliving those moments?

She got up, went to the bathroom, had a drink of water, and flopped down on her couch in front of the TV. She flipped through the channels. Nothing looked promising. It was all infomercials and late-night movies. The last thing she needed was a horror movie, so she settled on an advertisement for some sort of weird kitchen appliance. The drone of the TV guy's voice gradually calmed her nerves. Finally, a little after four, she felt able to flick off the television and crawl back into bed to grab a couple more hours of unhealthy sleep.

* * *

She climbed out of bed at her usual time, got dressed, and went for her morning run with Rolf. Then she had a quick shower, breakfast, and headed in to work. She had a lead to follow up. She couldn't afford to let herself think about the Russians anymore.

Some of the old-time knuckle-draggers at the NYPD liked to joke about female cops wanting to talk about makeup and clothes all the time, instead of dealing with the ugly side of police work. Erin was glad none of them were looking over her shoulder, because this was the first time she'd used a work computer to look up cosmetics.

She was trying to match the lipstick and perfume Janice Barnes had been wearing. Or at least, the lipstick and perfume that had been put on her body. She picked up her desk phone and called down to the morgue.

"Levine," the ME said when she finally picked up after five rings.

"This is O'Reilly up in Major Crimes," Erin said. "I have a question about cosmetics."

There was an awkward pause. "I think maybe you've reached the wrong department," Levine said at last.

"No, I wanted to ask you about putting makeup on a corpse."

"It's easy," Levine said. "Morticians do it all the time. Apparently some people find bodies off-putting without it. The lividity—"

"Is there any way to tell if makeup was applied to someone before or after they died?" Erin interrupted.

There was no answer. The silence went on long enough that Erin wondered if they'd been disconnected.

"Uh... Levine?"

"I'm thinking," Levine said. "Some cosmetics are liquid-based, so if they weren't completely dry when discovered, it might be possible to determine time of application. If you knew the precise time of death, you'd know whether the makeup had been applied ante- or post-mortem."

"But there's no way to know otherwise?"

"Not that I know of," Levine said. "I can check the literature. It's not normally a relevant question. Can I get back to work now?"

"Yeah, sure," Erin said. "Thanks."

Levine hung up without bothering to say goodbye.

Erin turned back to her computer screen. She had a pretty close match on the lipstick, she thought, but it was hard to tell.

Colors sometimes looked different on a computer than in real life, and there were more shades of red lipstick than she'd ever imagined. And of course the perfume wasn't something she could research online, at least until they developed scratch-and-sniff websites. It was probably just as well that those didn't exist, given the average American's Internet habits.

Levine had given her an idea, though, with her offhand remark about reaching the wrong department.

"Looks like it's a day of firsts," she said to Rolf. "We're going shopping on the clock."

*   *   *

Erin Googled the nearest perfume and cosmetic store. It was part of a chain of upscale New York shops, just down the street from the precinct. She decided to go on foot and give Rolf a little additional exercise. First, she went down to Evidence so Rolf could have a good sniff at Janice Barnes's dress. Then she gave him his search command and they went for their walk.

She was in luck. The store was empty except for the guy behind the counter. He was a clean-shaven man about her own age, good-looking, dark hair and very dark eyes. His name tag identified him as Trevor.

"Hello, ma'am," he said, giving her a warm, friendly smile. "What can I help you with today?"

"Hi, Trevor," she said. "I'm trying to track down a particular fragrance."

He glanced at Rolf, then back at her. "Ma'am, we don't usually allow dogs in the store," he said. "But for such a beautiful creature, I'll make an exception."

"He's a police K-9," she said, showing her shield. "I'm Detective O'Reilly."

His eyebrows rose slightly. "I see. Is this a business errand, or personal?"

"Business."

"That's a shame," he said. "You can't work all the time. A woman needs to take care of herself. Though I can see you do a good job of that. You're a very attractive woman, Detective. You shouldn't hide it."

"I'll keep that in mind," she said. "But right now, I'm looking for a perfume we found at a crime scene. Do you have samples on hand?"

"Of course. But we have dozens of different fragances. Are you planning on sorting through all possible perfumes by smell?"

"Not me," she said, pointing to Rolf.

He laughed. It sounded natural enough, but Erin thought it was just a little forced. "We've never had a dog try our samples before," he said. "But I suppose it's okay. They're over here." He went to a side counter and brought out a tray with a dizzying array of tiny bottles and labeled card samples.

"Let's get started," Erin said.

Trevor shrugged. As he began putting scented cards in front of Rolf, he watched Erin thoughtfully.

"What's the crime?" he asked.

"I can't discuss an ongoing investigation," she said absently, still looking at her dog.

"I might be able to help," he said. "Is it a female bank robber? A drag queen hitman?"

Erin was startled into a laugh. "No, nothing like that," she admitted. "Just trying to nail down some evidence."

"I see," Trevor said. "How will the dog know if it's the perfume you're looking for?"

"He's a trained search dog. I gave him a sample. He'll alert when he hits the right one." She sighed. "Assuming it's even here."

"He can track perfume?" Trevor said. "I thought they only knew to go after human smell."

"He'll track anything if I can give him a whiff of it," she said proudly. "Rolf is the best damn K-9 in New York."

"So once he has the scent, he'll be able to track down your target?"

"Absolutely," Erin said with more confidence than she felt. The trail was cold, and tracking a suspect through an urban area was tricky at the best of times, what with all the crisscrossing paths of millions of people.

"Amazing," he said. He set another row of cards down in front of Rolf, then turned to Erin again. "I'm sorry, I haven't properly introduced myself. Trevor Fairfax."

"Erin O'Reilly," Erin said, shaking hands. He had a firm grip, but soft hands. He held her hand just a little longer than politeness required. She had to make the first move to disengage.

"I've been working here almost ten years, and this is the first time I've had a policewoman come in on duty," he said. "I can suggest a couple of fragrances that would work great for you. You want to project power and confidence, right?"

"Not sure I need perfume for that," she said.

"Of course you don't need it," he said with a smile. "This store isn't about needs. We sell dreams and pleasures. Luxuries. Surely you can indulge in a little hedonism from time to time."

"Not often on my salary."

"Well, it looks like your dog came up empty," Trevor said. "He must be looking for something we don't have a sample for." He started to turn away.

"Hold on," Erin said. "I don't think he checked that batch on your right."

He paused. "Really?"

"You started with those," Erin said, pointing. "Set that bunch down for a sec, would you?"

He shrugged again and complied.

Rolf sneezed and shook his head, clearing some of the lingering bits of perfume from his nostrils, then snuffled at the sample cards. Immediately, as if a fishhook had grabbed his snout, he cranked his head to the side and took deep, heavy sniffs at the second card from the left in the assortment. Then he scratched at the card with his front paws.

"That's it," Erin said. She bent down to look at the sample card. "What's this one?"

"That's called Heartbreaker," Trevor said. "It's a lovely fragrance. Sensual, passionate, full of promise... with just a hint of tease to it. It's for the woman who wants to be beautiful but unattainable. You'd like it."

"I'm not gonna wear perfume that was put on a murder victim," Erin said without thinking.

"Murder?" Trevor echoed. "My God, that's terrible."

"Does your store keep sales records?" Erin said quickly, moving past her verbal slip.

"Of course."

"Are they just for your store, or for the whole chain?"

"Both," he said. "Corporate uses them to plot sales trends."

"I need to see them."

He hesitated. "I can't do that, Erin. I'm sorry. It's a customer privacy issue."

"I can get a court order."

He spread his hands apologetically. "Then I think you'd probably better do that," he said. "You don't want to overstep and get in trouble."

She gave him a sardonic half-smile. "Thanks for your concern."

"I really would like to help," he said. "I'll ask my manager about the sales records. Maybe he'll give me the go-ahead. And anything else I can do to help, you only have to ask."

"Thanks." She took out one of her cards and handed it to him. "Here's my phone number. Let me know as soon as you can about the sales info. Or anything else you can think of that might be helpful. Any strange guys buying this perfume, anything out of the ordinary."

"Of course," Trevor said. He offered his hand again. "Erin, it's been a pleasure to meet you. Please, don't hesitate if there's anything else you need."

She shook hands again. "Actually, there's one thing," she said. "I'll take a bottle of the Heartbreaker after all."

"Changed your mind?" he said, taking out a deep crimson bottle. "You won't be sorry. It's like a liquid dream."

"Hey," she said. "Remember the first rule of street dealing, Mr. Fairfax."

"What's that?"

"Never get high on your own supply."

He laughed. "I appreciate. I don't use. That'll be one hundred and five dollars."

"Holy shit!" Erin blurted out.

"It's worth it," he said. "Just give it a try."

"Okay," she said. It wasn't like she was buying it for personal use. This was going to be expensed to the department. She just hoped the price tag didn't give Webb a coronary.

Trevor expertly bundled the little bottle into a dark red gift bag. Erin handed over her credit card, making sure to get the receipt in the bag.

"Okay, you're all set," he said.

"Thanks, Mr. Fairfax. You've been very helpful."

"Any time, Detective," he said with a smile, looking her straight in the eye. "I hope to see you again sometime. Then you can tell me I'm right about the Heartbreaker."

"Like a liquid dream," she said, wondering what kind of dream it'd turn out to be.

Chapter 8

When Erin got back to Precinct 8, the others were gathered around the whiteboard. They'd been updating it with all the information they'd been able to collect regarding the double shooting. Unfortunately, there were a lot of holes. Jones had printed out some blank silhouettes to use in place of photos for guys they couldn't ID. There was a line from an outline labeled "Smiling Jack" through the *Loch Druich* to New York, ending in another outline labeled "Receiver." Jones had written "C4?" by a copy of the cargo manifest. Another line intersected the first one at the ship, with yet another blank portrait representing the pirate. Under him was the one word "German?"

"How's it going?" Erin asked.

Vic grunted. He didn't look happy.

Webb glanced at her. "It's starting to come together," he said. Then he saw the gift bag in her hand. "What's that?"

"Perfume."

"Please tell me you haven't been visiting boutiques on your coffee break."

"It's case-related," she said. "Rolf matched it to the perfume on the hotel victim."

"Really?" Jones said, walking to meet her. "Let me take a whiff."

"Careful," Erin said. "It's expensive."

"I can't wait for the annual departmental budget review," Webb muttered.

"Bury it in the equipment and uniform budget," Vic suggested.

Erin opened the bottle. Jones sniffed at it.

"Okay," she said. "What is it?"

"It's called Heartbreaker," Erin said.

"Exotic?" Webb asked.

"Not really," she said. "Just pricy. There's at least half a dozen outlets where you could buy it in Manhattan alone, not counting the Internet. We could go for a court order for the sales, but if the guy paid cash, it won't help us trace him."

"Then what's the good of it?" Vic asked.

Erin knew it was important, but she wasn't quite sure why. "I'm building a picture of the killer," she said at last. "Trying to figure him out."

"Oh, good," Webb said. "You're a profiler now. You looking to transfer to the Bureau, become a Feebie?"

"Just trying to catch this son of a bitch."

"Okay, profile him," Webb said, putting his hands on his hips. "Why'd this mystery man kill this girl?"

"Same reason most ser—" she began, then caught herself. "Same reason guys like that always kill girls. For the thrill of it."

"Psychological gratification," Jones put in. "Usually in cases like these, the killer either strangles his victim or uses a blade." She shivered. "It's more intimate that way."

"Poison's a little odd, wouldn't you say?" Webb asked.

Erin nodded. "I think... I think he doesn't actually like doing anything physical to his victims," she said. "Janice Barnes wasn't raped. No bruises or ligature marks. He was really careful not to mess her up. It's almost like he just wanted to look at her, and killing her was incidental."

"An aesthetic murderer," Webb said. He shook his head. "That's a stretch, O'Reilly."

"It explains the way he posed her, dressed her up, put makeup on her," she argued. "I'll bet he actually thinks he admires women. He may even think he's doing them a favor."

"Putting us on pedestals," Jones said. "That's really creepy."

"Look," Webb said. "I can see you're sold on this, but I'm not. I'm not saying you're wrong. But you need more. I want you to keep digging, but we've got a bigger problem at the moment. If you're right about the missing cargo from the *Loch Druich*, we need to find it. I'm not sure we've got time to run down both cases."

"We could punt this over to Homeland Security, take it Federal," Vic suggested.

"Hell, Neshenko, you could take early retirement," Webb snapped. "Then you wouldn't have to work any more cases, ever."

"That's not what I meant," Vic said.

"Sir, maybe Vic's right," Jones said. "If this guy's a foreign national and he's brought explosives into New York, that's exactly what Homeland Security is for."

"Yeah, because the Feds did such a great job protecting New York from terrorists in the past," Webb said.

"Not sure the NYPD did any better," Vic said.

Erin took a step toward him, clenching her fists at her sides. "My dad was on the force on 9/11," she said. "I know guys who died that day. What the hell is your problem?"

Jones got between them. "Whoa," she said. "He didn't mean anything."

Vic scowled, but something in her look seemed to get through to him. He dropped his eyes. "Sorry," he said. "That was outta line."

Erin backed off and relaxed her hands.

"The point," Webb said, "is that Homeland Security will go berserk if we call them in. They'll do more harm than good. Let's keep this quiet for now, at least until we know who we're looking for."

"What if the C4 wasn't the point?" Jones said suddenly.

Everyone turned to look at her.

"What?" she said. "It's just a question."

"It was a robbery," Webb said, speaking as if he was explaining a very simple concept to a recent Academy graduate. "They tortured these guys to find out where the explosives were, then they killed them and dumped them."

"We're assuming the only questions this German guy asked were about the cargo," Jones said, but she faltered as she said it.

"What else would he have been asking?" Webb asked.

"I don't know," Jones said. "What else did Carr and Garrity know?"

"Depends who they were working for," Vic said.

Webb looked back at the whiteboard. He poked Smiling Jack with his finger. "Neshenko, we need to know who this guy is, and how he's connected. Get back on the phone with Interpol."

"Shit," Vic growled. "I knew it. I goddamn knew you were gonna say that. I hate talking to those guys." He picked up his phone. "If I'm still on hold by this time next week, send help."

"We have any idea who their contact was in New York?" Jones asked.

Webb shook his head. "It's apparently a pretty disciplined organization. Good compartmentalization. MacIntosh says he doesn't know who they were delivering to."

"You believe him?" Erin asked.

Webb shrugged. "No reason not to. He spilled on everything else I asked. I'll take another run at him anyway, see if I can shake any recollections loose."

"It okay if I grab a bite?" Erin asked. It was after 1:30. They'd forgotten about lunch, and her stomach was growling.

"Sure," Webb said.

"I'll come with you," Jones offered.

"Okay," Erin said. "Let's go."

*　　*　　*

They went to a Chinese place just down the street. Erin had long ago learned that savvy takeout owners set up shop as close to police precincts as possible. Erin got General Tso's Chicken and Jones ordered vegetarian fried rice. Rolf was too proud to beg for table scraps, so he'd have to wait for his kibble. They decided to eat at the restaurant instead of doing carryout. Neither was keen to dash back to the precinct right away.

"So," Jones said once they were sitting down over their meal. "How are you holding up?"

"I'm fine," Erin said automatically.

"Really?" Jones said. "Because I keep having nightmares about that fight under the train tracks." She laughed nervously. "I swear to God, I've never been so scared in my life."

"Jones, it's okay," Erin said. "They were shooting at us. Of course we were scared."

"Hey, Erin, we've been working together a while now. Kira's fine."

"Sure, Kira. You holding things together?"

Kira snorted. "Well, you know how it goes. How you doing?"

"Okay," Erin replied. "But there's something with the Lieutenant. He's a good enough cop, but he can be such a jackass sometimes. It's like he's decided, ever since the goddamn Russians, I'm this fragile bundle of nerves that's got no business being on the street."

Kira's eyes narrowed. "You really think that? Why?"

"Hell, yes," Erin said. She took a bite of her chicken and chewed it angrily. "I can do fantastic police work, and he just keeps riding me. He's sure I've got PTSD, that I'm weak, that I'm incompetent. He doesn't believe a word I'm saying about this murder, and—"

"Girl, can you even hear yourself?" Kira interrupted. "You are so full of shit."

Erin stopped short, mouth hanging open in surprise.

"Look, I'm your friend, right?" Kira demanded.

"Yeah, I guess so."

"So I'm gonna give you a reality check. 'Cause that's what friends do. Yeah, Webb's a medium-large asshole sometimes, but you think he doesn't trust you? Erin, he's got you working point on your own case. You think he's given that to me? Or to Vic?"

Dumbfounded, Erin didn't have an answer.

"Damn it, Erin, I'd give my left pinkie to be doing what you're doing. You've got a chance to solve your case, a major goddamn case, and you're bitching because the LT is hurting your feelings? Listen, don't make him righter than he ought to be. Don't go all emotional on us."

"Emotional?" Erin echoed. "But you just said—"

"Yeah, I know," Kira said. She stared down at her fried rice and poked at it with her chopsticks. "I'm an emotional creature, too. Look, Erin, every morning I have to pull my shit together before I can even get out of bed and come in to work. I'm scared basically all the time, just plain scared half out of my mind. I don't know how you do it. I don't know how anybody does. But we show up, so we have to bring our A-game. We have to be tougher than we think we are, because otherwise we're going to fall to fucking pieces. So don't you start with me, because I need you strong."

Erin stared across the table. She saw that Kira was actually fighting tears. "Jesus," she said. "I'm sorry. I—I didn't know."

Kira looked up at her. "No, I'm sorry. It's not fair to lay all that on you. This is my shit, and I've got to deal with it."

Erin nodded. She could respect that. "Hey, if you do need anything," she said awkwardly.

"I'll call in a 10-13," Kira said with a wan smile. "It's just... Erin, you're on the fast track here and all you're seeing is the bullshit that's getting in your way. And me, I'm not sure I can do this at all. Maybe I should go back to Internal Affairs, ride a desk. At least there, no one's going to shoot at me."

"You sleeping okay?" Erin asked.

"Hell no. I'm taking pills for it."

"Bad dreams every night?"

"Yeah. You?"

"Pretty much."

They ate in silence for a few minutes.

"So, you following the Yankees?" Erin asked finally.

"Erin," Kira said, "You have a lot of brothers, don't you."

Erin laughed. "That obvious, huh?"

"It shows."

"We could talk fashion instead, or boy bands," Erin suggested. "That girly enough for you?"

Kira shuddered. "Or perfume," she said. "Maybe fingernails."

"You're morbid."

"Least I'm not girly," Kira shot back.

"What do you think those two guys were tortured for?" Erin asked.

"Information."

"Yeah, but what information?"

Kira thought it over. "When I was with the gang task force, I remember how they handled things. When you're breaking up a gang, you can't start at the top. Usually, you don't even know who's calling the shots. So you get some lower-ranking guys and flip them. They don't know much, but they can give you the next guy up the food chain. Then you follow it to the top."

"You think someone was using these guys just to get to their boss?" Erin asked. "That's pretty cold."

Kira shrugged. "We're talking about a guy who ripped their fingernails off, then shot them and dumped them overboard. I'm not thinking we're looking for a real sensitive, touchy-feely kind of guy."

"Right," Erin said. She chased her last piece of chicken around her plate.

"Of course, knowing what they're after doesn't help us find the killers," Kira said. "Maybe Vic can turn up something on the dead guys' organization."

"Yeah," Erin said, but she wasn't really listening. She was thinking about criminal hierarchies and the New York underworld, and wondering if she should pull on some of the threads she already had hold of, see what came loose.

"Hey," Kira said, waving a hand in front of Erin's nose. "Come in, Officer."

Erin blinked. "I need to go talk to someone."

"This for the hotel case, or the boat?"

"The boat." Erin stood up. "I'll meet you back at the precinct."

"Where you going?"

"To talk to a CI."

"Be careful."

"I'm always careful."

"That's not comforting, given our track record."

"Hey," Erin said. "I've got this."

Chapter 9

The lunchtime rush had ended by the time Erin and Rolf got to the Barley Corner. The pub was almost deserted. One waitress, Danny the bartender, a pair of young toughs, and Carlyle were the only people present. The two guys wore white wife-beaters that showed off Celtic tattoos on their shoulders. They gave Erin a once-over. She stared coolly back. They took in the shield at her belt and the K-9 at her side and immediately looked away, pretending to ignore her. She marked them as street-level wiseguys as easily as they'd made her as a cop.

Carlyle stood up to greet her, as he always did. "Erin, darling. Come, sit down."

She took a seat at the counter to Carlyle's left. Danny drifted over.

"Get you something, ma'am?"

She shook her head. "Not now, Danny. I'm on the clock."

"It's business, then," Carlyle said. "But it's always a pleasure to welcome you here, business or no. Come, you surely want something to wet your throat, if we're to be talking. Corky would suggest a virgin Rum-and-Coke."

"So... that'd be a Coke?" Erin asked, raising her eyebrows.

"If you insist."

"I don't know what's more ridiculous," she said. "That Corky would ever order anything without alcohol, or that you'd mention him and 'virgin' in the same sentence."

Carlyle laughed. "Fair points."

"I don't see him in here," she said, glancing around again.

"He's a working lad, with his living to make."

"Well, don't tell him I said hello. It'll just encourage him."

"You're a woman to break an Irishman's heart," he said, smiling.

"I didn't come here to break anyone's heart," she replied.

"No, I imagine you came to pick my brain."

She nodded.

"So what are you wanting to be knowing?" he asked

"Smiling Jack."

His face gave nothing away. "I beg your pardon?"

"Smiling Jack," she repeated. "Gangster. Scars on his cheeks."

"A great many gangsters have scars. It's not the safest of occupations."

"You know who moves product into New York," she said. "You're plugged into the networks."

"And you're trying to find this cheerful lad?"

"I don't think he's very cheerful," she said. "And I know where he is. Glasgow."

"Ah," Carlyle said. "I fail to see how he's your concern, in that case."

"I don't care about him," she said. "But someone else does, and that's who I'm trying to find."

"I don't think I'm following you."

"Jack had a shipment coming into New York," she said. "On the *Loch Druich*."

Carlyle waited, watching her face.

"There were two guys on board the ship," she went on. "Garrity and Carr. You ever heard of them?"

"Those aren't exactly uncommon names among folk of Celtic extraction," Carlyle said. "What is it you're seeking them for?"

"I'm not looking for them, either. I know where they are, too."

Carlyle spread his hands. "Then I'm afraid we find ourselves in an uncharacteristic position, Erin. I'd say you know a great deal more than I. Frankly, I don't see how I can assist you. Where are these lads you mentioned?"

"We've got them back at the station," she said, telling a technical truth.

"Then perhaps they're the ones you should be asking these questions."

"I don't think they'd have much to say."

Their eyes were locked on each other, both looking for more information than their words conveyed. Carlyle nodded ever so slightly.

"Perhaps not," he agreed. "I take it something untoward has occurred."

Erin broke eye contact while she tried to think what to say next. Her gaze traveled across the bottles behind the bar. A familiar label caught her eye.

She looked back at Carlyle. "On second thought, I think I'll take you up on that drink."

"Ah, grand," he said, signaling to the bartender. "Danny, whatever this young lady wants, on the house of course."

"A whiskey," she said. "Glen D. And leave the bottle."

Danny blinked, then grinned. "Glad to, ma'am. Take it slow, though." He poured her drink and set the bottle on the counter beside the glass.

She picked the bottle up and examined it, holding it up so

the light shone through the amber liquid. "You know," she said to Carlyle, "I've never seen this brand of whiskey anywhere but here."

"It's a small label," he said. "Hand-crafted in the Highlands according to a thousand-year-old recipe, or so I'm told."

"Glen Docherty-Kinlochewe," she said slowly. "Am I saying that right?"

"I've no idea," he said. "I'm Irish, not Scottish."

"It's a funny thing," Erin said, still speaking slowly and quietly. "The *Loch Druich* had some cases of Glen D on her manifest. And here, talking to you, I've got another bottle of the stuff. Would you call that a coincidence?"

"Does it matter what I'd call it?" he replied.

"Look, Cars," she said, abandoning her coyness. "You and I both know what was in those cases on that ship. Just like you knew about the two guys who were coming in to keep an eye on that cargo. There's things you won't tell me, sure. But we have to talk about this, because someone killed Garrity and Carr for what they knew, and I don't think they're gonna stop there. If we're gonna put a stop to this before it goes any further, I need your help."

Carlyle took a moment, thinking it over. "I'd like to invite you to my office," he said. "If you'd care to step upstairs, we can speak with a touch more privacy."

"I think that's a good idea," Erin said.

He got up. "If you'll follow me, darling. Feel free to bring your drink with you."

"I didn't really want it," she admitted.

"And you call yourself an Irishwoman," he said, shaking his head sadly. He picked up the bottle and the glass. "I'll bring these along. Either you'll decide you want it after all, or I'll see it doesn't go to waste."

*   *   *

Carlyle's apartment was directly above the Corner, reached by a door at the back of the bar. Erin couldn't help noticing the door was steel-core and a good two inches thick. She raised her eyebrows and cocked her head at it.

"Soundproofing," he said. "The lads get a mite rowdy of a night, and I need a bit of sleep now and again."

He led her up a flight of stairs to an upstairs hallway. To her surprise, she saw that the entire floor was a single suite of rooms. The thought of the cost of that much Manhattan real estate made her eyes water.

The place was furnished with high-quality furniture, but nothing ostentatious. Carlyle was clearly a man who liked nice things, but wasn't showy about it. Everything was neat and clean, no clutter at all.

He ushered her into his private office. It was finished in dark wood paneling with a heavy-looking mahogany desk, a leather swivel chair, and a couple of armchairs in the corner, a floor lamp between them. Except for the laptop computer on the desk, the whole room might've been lifted out of the nineteenth century.

Carlyle turned on the lamp. Warm, golden light filled the room.

"Please," he said, motioning her to one of the armchairs. He sat in the other, facing her. Rolf lay down beside Erin and rested his chin on his front paws.

"This is where you do business, huh?" she asked.

"Nay, darling," he said with a smile. "Most of my business is conducted downstairs. This is where I balance the accounts, or share a quiet drink with a friend."

"Is that what we are? Friends?"

"Aren't we?"

"Anyone ever tell you you've got a habit of answering questions with other questions?"

"You think so?"

She had to laugh. He was smooth, that was for sure. No wonder he'd never even been charged with a crime. Nothing stuck to him. She reminded herself that for all that, he was a member of a powerful underworld organization. The O'Malleys were no laughing matter. And that was why she was here.

"You knew Carr and Garrity," she said. It wasn't a question.

"What happened to these lads you speak of?" he replied. It wasn't an answer.

"You know a guy with a German accent who might want to go after them?"

"German, you say?" Carlyle repeated, and for the first time, his eyes gave something away.

"Yeah, German," Erin said. "Acts like a pirate. Doesn't shy away from killing. Ring any bells?"

"Rüdel," Carlyle said quietly.

"Who's that?"

"A lad I've heard of, from time to time," he said. "I'd heard he might be in the neighborhood."

"Tell me about him."

"I've not met the man," Carlyle said. He was still holding the glass of whiskey. He tossed it back in a single swallow, not even flinching at the burn in his throat. "I've only heard stories, you ken."

"What do these stories say?"

"He's a lad who does piecework for hire. A mercenary of sorts. He specializes in what the corporate lads call hostile takeovers."

"What does he take over?"

"Organizations."

"Like the O'Malleys."

"Organizations which operate beyond the restrictions of the law," Carlyle said. "Which I'm not saying Evan O'Malley has anything to do with, mind. What you have to know is how rare such a man is."

"How do you mean?"

Carlyle poured himself another shot of Glen D, but didn't drink it right away. He stared into the glass while he talked. "These organizations are like any other company, Erin. They're run like every business, and for the same goal."

"To make money," she said.

"Aye. If they could make more money operating within the law, they'd do that, and I imagine your lot would have to find some other use for your time. But the point is, there are businesses taking in money, all across this fair city of ours, every day. In quantities so vast it beggars the imagination. They've no fondness for complications. Believe it or not, with a few psychopathic exceptions, organization lads have no interest in violence or killing. They're willing to do it, of course, but they'd rather not. Blood is expensive and messy. It brings all manner of complications and attention."

"But this Rüdel?" she prompted.

"He's purely a fighter," Carlyle said. "The bloodshed and violence other lads avoid, he seeks out. He's the lad they call in when someone's determined to pile up a great many bodies."

"Carlyle," Erin said. "Were Garrity and Carr connected with the O'Malleys?"

He gave her a long, level look. "I like you, Erin," he said. "And I liked your father. You're both good coppers, and I respect that. Leaving that aside, you saved my life, and my place of business. But there's things you shouldn't ask an Irishman to do, and foremost among them is to rat out his fellows. So please, don't ask me questions you know I'll not answer."

She sighed. "This Rüdel, if that's who it was, shot Garrity

and Carr. We're trying to catch a killer. If these were your guys, we're on the same side here. Anything you can tell me might help us put this thing to rest." She paused, then decided the hell with it, she'd tell him. "They were tortured before they were killed. Depending on what they knew, any of their associates might be in danger."

At that moment a series of muffled popping sounds came through the floor, like distant champagne corks, or maybe someone squeezing a handful of bubble wrap.

"I thought you said this place was soundproofed," she said.

"It is."

A thrill of adrenaline rushed through Erin's body. She jumped to her feet. "Was that gunfire?"

"That bit about the torture," Carlyle said dryly, "would have been a fine piece of information with which to begin our conversation."

Erin already had her phone out and was calling Dispatch. "This is O'Reilly, shield four-six-four-oh. I have a 10-13S at the Barley Corner pub. All available units."

"Ten-four, O'Reilly," Dispatch replied. "Stand by."

Erin turned to Carlyle. "Jesus Christ," she said. "He's coming after *you*."

Chapter 10

The gunfire downstairs hadn't lasted long. Everything was quiet now. Erin had seen the thickness of the door to Carlyle's apartment. It would hold against anything short of a missile launcher. Backup was inbound. All they had to do was sit tight and the cavalry would arrive in five minutes at most, maybe less.

Except she couldn't do that. There were civilians downstairs. She'd counted four people in the pub when they'd gone up. Some might be wounded. Some might be uninjured but still in danger. It wasn't her job to duck and cover when bullets started flying. Cops were supposed to go toward the sound of the shooting.

She drew her Glock and press-checked it to make sure a round was chambered. "Stay here," she said to Carlyle. "Lock the door behind me."

"Bugger that," Carlyle said. His face had gone very rigid, but he remained outwardly calm. "I'll watch your back."

She didn't have time for this. "No!" she snapped, stepping into the hallway and angling for the stairs. "Keep out of this. You're a civilian!"

He was right behind her. "Nay," he said with surprising gentleness, "I'm not. And those are my own people down there."

"Damn it," she growled, "stay behind this door. That's an order!"

She dropped a hand to Rolf's collar, getting ready to unsnap his leash. The Shepherd had picked up on her mood. His hackles rose on his neck. He was ready.

Carlyle was saying something else, still arguing. She ignored him. Her heart pounded in her ears. She went over the layout of the pub in her head, trying to remember who'd been sitting in which seats, where there was good cover, where she'd go.

She was about halfway down the stairs when the door exploded.

There wasn't time to duck, to say anything, to think. All she saw was a bright flash. Then a giant invisible hand slapped her entire body and flung her back against the stairs. Her head smacked against the corner of one of the steps. She didn't hear the explosion. She didn't hear anything at all. She felt a high-pitched thrumming vibration in her eardrums.

Erin couldn't tell which way was up. Sunbursts flashed in front of her eyes. The only sense that seemed to be working properly was her sense of smell. She smelled smoke and something hot and coppery.

Breaching charge, she thought disjointedly. Something was supposed to happen right afterward. Something important.

She was moving. It felt like falling, except she was moving up instead of down. That didn't make any sense. She tried to clear her head.

Then she remembered where she was. Someone had his hands under her arms and was hauling her up the stairs backward. Someone else was in the doorway below, a stocky guy wearing a ski mask. He was holding some sort of gun.

Erin tried to shout, to identify herself as NYPD, but her ears still weren't working right. She didn't know if any sound came out of her mouth or not. It didn't matter. The man was clearly about to shoot her.

She raised her right hand. Her Glock was still in it, somehow. She wrapped her other hand around the grip, aimed between her own feet, and pulled the trigger three times.

The shock of the recoil traveled up her arms. She heard the gunshots, as if they were coming from a great distance. Her hearing must be coming back, she thought distractedly.

But her inner ear still wasn't up to snuff. The range was less than fifteen feet, and the target didn't go down. Her shooting instructor would've chewed her ass out for missing at that distance. She'd given the perp something to think about, though. He ducked back behind the doorframe.

Then she was in the upstairs hallway again, with no clear idea of how she'd gotten there. The person who'd dragged her up had let go of her. Two faces were peering down at her. One was black and furry, with very large, pointed ears. The other was a silver-haired man. Both looked anxious.

"Erin!"

She heard Carlyle, faintly, and sat up. She almost fell back down again, but managed to stay half upright. She pointed her gun at the stairwell. No one had come up the stairs yet.

Carlyle was kneeling beside her, asking her a question. She forced herself to focus.

"What do you need?" he repeated.

"Get your gun," she said, forming her words carefully. There was something wet on her upper lip. She licked it and tasted blood. Her nose must be bleeding.

"I don't keep a gun," he said.

She couldn't believe it. Trapped with the only unarmed mobster in New York.

A staccato burst of gunfire tore into the plaster at the top of the stairs. The attackers were using submachine-guns. They were also using military-style tactics, which meant one of them was laying down covering fire while at least one more moved forward. Erin had seconds before bad guys would be swarming up the stairs.

"Get my extra piece," she told Carlyle. "Right ankle."

Carlyle bent forward and slid his hand up her lower leg, finding the gun and pulling it free. It was an oddly intimate touch, Erin thought, then told herself to get her shit together and think clearly. Carlyle knelt next to her, holding the tiny pocket-pistol in both hands.

The blunt muzzle of a submachine-gun poked around the corner. Muzzle flashes flared, the unseen gunman sweeping the hallway. Then the man charged. But he'd aimed at chest height. Erin was sitting down and Carlyle was crouched low. He'd fired too high.

Erin's reflexes were better than Carlyle's, even dazed as she was. Her first shot clipped the attacker high up on the shoulder. He was knocked halfway around and her next bullet whipped past him. Then Carlyle fired. His bullet smashed into the gunman's right arm just above the elbow. The submachine-gun dropped to the floor.

Erin very nearly shot the masked man again out of sheer instinct. But she hesitated when she saw his empty hands. He was clutching his arm, hunched over in pain.

"Get down on the floor!" she shouted.

He didn't move.

"Get down, or I'll shoot you in the goddamn face!" she yelled at him. Another guy was likely to come up the stairs any moment, and she wanted a clear field of fire when he did.

"*Was sagen Sie?*" the man said through gritted teeth.

"I'm not certain he speaks English," Carlyle said in Erin's ear.

Erin shifted gears. "*Sitz!*" she shouted at the man, gesturing with her pistol. "*Bleib!*"

The guy looked startled, in spite of his pain. He sat down immediately and heavily, still clutching his arm. Rolf, almost equally surprised, did the same.

Erin and Carlyle kept their guns trained down the hallway. Seconds passed.

Nothing happened.

"You know German?" Carlyle asked after several endless moments. His tone was light and conversational. Her hearing was definitely coming back.

"Rolf's from Germany," she said, neither of them looking away from the stairwell while they talked. "It was easier to train me than to retrain him."

"Ah," Carlyle said. "I fear I've never learned a foreign tongue. Unless, of course, you count American English."

"Depends what part of America," Erin said, thinking this was a pretty strange thing to be talking about.

"Do you think any other lads will be coming upstairs?" he asked.

"You know these guys better than I do," she replied.

They heard sirens outside, closing rapidly.

"I'm thinking they've gone," Carlyle said. "Lads like that don't hang about when the coppers come calling. Perhaps you should send your loyal hound in pursuit?"

Erin shook her head. "He's not wearing his vest," she said. She got her feet under her and stood up, still a little shaky. Carlyle, ever the gentleman, rose alongside her and offered his arm. She leaned on him for a second while she got her balance. "Those assholes have automatic weapons," she added. "I'm not sending Rolf on his own."

From downstairs, through the open doorway, came the shouts of "NYPD!" From the sound of it, two or three units had arrived.

"NYPD!" Erin shouted back. "Upstairs clear! I've got one in custody! We'll need a bus." She walked slowly down the hall to the wounded man and kicked the fallen gun away from him. She didn't know the German words for what she wanted him to do, but a little gunpoint pantomime got the message across. He lay down on his stomach. She frisked him and found a Sig-Sauer automatic pistol in his belt. She took it away from him.

After ensuring the prisoner posed no immediate threat, Erin turned to Carlyle. "I'm gonna need my gun back," she said. She was already trying to think how she'd explain this in her report. She'd given a police firearm to a known associate of a major criminal organization.

He reversed the pistol and extended it to her, grip-first. "It's just as well," he said. "I'm no great hand with a revolver."

As she took her backup weapon, she saw the sleeve of his gray suit coat was torn. "You had a close call there," she said. Then she saw the dark stain on the shirt underneath. "Shit. You've been hit!"

Carlyle looked down at his arm. "Aye, it seems I have."

"Why didn't you say something?"

"You'd a great deal with which to concern yourself," he said. "It's not bad, I'm thinking. Hardly more than a scratch."

Then he went pale and leaned against the wall as the excitement of the fight started to drain out of him. "Perhaps I'll sit for a moment, if it's no bother," he said.

Three uniformed officers rushed up the stairs. Erin held up her shield.

"That's one of them," she said, pointing to the downed gunman.

"What about him?" one of the patrolmen asked, pointing to Carlyle.

"He's the owner," she said. "Get that damn bus here!" She turned her full attention to Carlyle. "Let's have a look at that arm."

"Never mind the arm," he said. "What about my people?"

"We've got two dead downstairs," a patrolman said with unthinking harshness.

Erin thought of Danny the bartender, with his cheerful smile. "Who?" she said through a mouth gone suddenly dry.

"Couple of wiseguys," another officer said. "Lots of ink on their arms, both of them strapped. One got his piece out, but looks like he never got the chance to use it."

Carlyle closed his eyes and said nothing.

"What about the others?" Erin asked.

"What others?" the first patrolman replied. "I didn't see anyone else. We came straight up. We got more uniforms downstairs, clearing the place. They ought to know."

"Hold still," Erin said to Carlyle. He was trying to push past the police to the stairs. "You're bleeding and you're gonna make it worse."

"The sooner you let me see to my folk, the sooner I'll let you see to my arm," he retorted.

The injury wasn't bleeding all that heavily, as far as Erin could see, and unless she was prepared to manhandle him, the best thing to do was probably to figure out what had happened to the rest of the Corner's population.

"Detective, you're bleeding, too," an officer said, pointing to her face.

She wiped at her upper lip. Her fingers came away with a smear of red.

"Nosebleed," she said. "I'm fine."

"Look at that," the second officer said. "Your dog's got one, too. Never seen a dog with a nosebleed."

It was true. Rolf had a slow leak going from his nostrils. He swiped his snout clean with his tongue and looked at her for further instructions, apparently unconcerned.

Leaving her wounded prisoner with the patrol officers, Erin went downstairs with Carlyle and Rolf. She wondered what sort of war zone she'd find. From the size of the explosion that'd blown in the door, she expected the bar to look like an artillery shell had hit it.

She was mistaken. The door was blasted open, a jagged hole torn clean through it where the lock had been. The hinges were twisted and bent, but the rest of the room had taken remarkably little damage. The bar appeared totally intact, with the exception of a cluster of bullet holes in one of the booths. Two bodies were sprawled there, white tank tops soaked with blood.

More NYPD reinforcements had arrived. Seven officers were milling around, examining the scene. Two were talking to Danny and the waitress, who appeared unharmed. Erin's heart leaped with relief at the sight of them. The waitress was clutching Danny's arm just above the elbow, leaning against him for physical and moral support.

"So what did you see, Miss Tierney?" one of the cops asked her.

"I was behind the bar when they came in," she said. "Ned... Ned had ordered a pint of Guinness. Danny was pouring it for me. I didn't see them, but Danny did, over my shoulder. He dropped the glass on the floor." She pointed behind the bar. Erin glanced over and saw a pool of spilled stout, studded with shards of broken glass.

"He just grabbed me and pulled me down," the girl continued. "He lay on top of me. I wanted to yell at him, but he'd knocked the wind out of me. By the time I could talk, there was... shooting. They... they shot Ned and... and Vern." She paused, making an effort to steady her voice. "Danny held me down and we didn't make a sound. Some men were talking in some other language, German I think. Then there was a really loud bang and more shooting. After that, I heard a couple of guys running. They went out the back."

"How many of these men were there, total?" the officer asked.

"I saw three," Danny said.

"Could you identify them?"

He shook his head. "They were wearing masks."

The waitress looked up at him with undisguised admiration. "Danny didn't even cut me on the broken glass," she said. "He saved my life."

"Caitlin's exaggerating," he said. "Anybody would've done the same thing. We were lucky." Danny spoke calmly, but his hands were shaking.

Erin briefly considered going after the departed bad guys. Rolf could track them as long as they were on foot. But there'd be time for that in a little while, and besides, they'd almost certainly hopped into a getaway car. Right now, she had a wounded man to attend to. "Okay, Carlyle," she said to him. "There's nothing else you can do for your people right now. Take off that coat."

She managed to maneuver him to a table and sit him down. He took off his suit coat. Underneath, he wore a white silk shirt and a dark charcoal necktie. The shirtsleeve was torn and bloody.

"The shirt, too," she said.

"Erin, darling," he said. "Under other circumstances, that's an invitation a great many lads might welcome." He loosened the knot of his tie and began unbuttoning his shirt.

"Not tonight," she shot back with a grim smile. "I'm not in the mood."

He smiled at her and gingerly eased his wounded arm out of its sleeve. He was in excellent condition, and not just for a guy pushing fifty. His chest and shoulders were lean but well-muscled. The effect was a little spoiled by the blood running down his right bicep. Erin carefully probed his arm with her fingertips. The bullet had torn a furrow along the outside of his upper arm, missing the bone.

"You're gonna be fine," she said, giving him what she hoped was a reassuring smile. "It didn't hit anything but meat, in and out. You'll just want a few stitches on this. Couple of weeks, you'll be doing pushups again."

"Now just what am I interrupting?" a voice exclaimed from the doorway in a thick Irish brogue.

Erin's head whipped around. James Corcoran, Corky to his friends, stood just inside the pub.

"For Christ's sake!" a police sergeant exclaimed. "Jacoby, I told you to secure the goddamn perimeter!"

The officer in question gave his sergeant a helpless shrug. "I dunno how he got past me, Sarge."

"Well, get him the hell out of here!" the sergeant snapped. "This is a crime scene!"

"I'll say it is," Corky said, scanning Erin and the half-clad Carlyle. "It appears I've stumbled on all manner of depravity." As Officer Jacoby made a grab for him, he sidestepped so quickly and neatly it looked almost like a dance move. "I was in the neighborhood, Cars. Everything under control? I see Ned and Vern copped it."

"We'll talk later, Corks," Carlyle said.

"God damn it!" the sergeant shouted, making a move toward Corky. "Outside. Now!"

"I understand," Corky said, giving Erin a very suggestive wink. "Some things, a lass needs her privacy."

Erin was still trying to think of a stinging retort as Corky slipped back out of the Corner, closely pursued by two police, but somehow managing to make it look like leaving was his own idea.

Erin looked at Carlyle. There was a second of silence. Then both of them started laughing, with only a hint of hysteria.

The patrol officers looked at one another and shook their heads. There was just no accounting for detectives.

Chapter 11

"Remember the last time we were all in this bar together?" Webb demanded. He had his hands on his hips, a smoldering cigarette poking out from between two of his fingers.

"Yes, sir," Erin said.

"It was pretty much the same, am I right?" Webb went on. "Jones. Jog my memory. No, wait. Never mind. I know the difference. Last time, the bomb didn't go off. This time it did. Oh, and this time there's two bodies, a hospital case, and an officer-involved shooting. Am I missing anything?"

It didn't seem like a good time to speak up, so Erin didn't.

"Lieutenant, I'm merely grateful Detective O'Reilly was present," Carlyle said. The EMTs had bandaged up his flesh wound and he'd put on a clean shirt and tie. He was calm again, polite, and pleasant. "She saved not merely my own life, but Caitlin's and Danny's as well. I'd like to extend my personal gratitude to the New York Police Department."

Vic's snort let the room know what he thought of Carlyle's personal gratitude.

The rest of the squad had turned up as soon as news of the shootout percolated through the Dispatch network. They joined the paramedics, a whole lot of Patrol officers, and the recently-arrived Bomb Squad.

"Hey, Erin," the bomb tech said, raising a hand.

"Hey, Skip." She gave him a wave, glad of the momentary diversion from her pissed-off commanding officer.

Skip Taylor was a former bomb-disposal soldier. He'd talked Erin through defusing a homemade bomb at the Corner earlier that summer. He was way more cheerful than anybody had a right to be when their job involved taking apart booby traps and explosive devices.

"Hey, Cars, how's it going?" Skip said, extending a hand. Carlyle smiled and shook with him. Skip knew all about Carlyle's history with the IRA. It didn't make him hate the Irishman. Instead, he treated Carlyle with the courtesy and respect of one professional to another.

"What've we got here?" Skip continued, walking over to the blasted door. "Shaped charge, looks like. It's a breaching charge, absolutely."

"Certainly," Carlyle agreed. He stood just behind Skip and to one side, watching with interest. Webb glared at them but didn't interrupt.

"No sign of casing fragments," Skip said. "I'd say plastic explosive." He put on his gloves and opened his equipment case, pulling out a sample kit. He swabbed several surfaces on and around the door. "Remote detonation?"

"Wire," Carlyle said, pointing. A thin filament of copper, bright and shiny, lay just around the corner by the restrooms.

"Good eye," Skip said. "What do you figure?"

"The lads likely laid their charge, then went into the washroom," Carlyle said. "They'd be protected from the blast there, in case their shaping of the charge didn't go precisely as planned."

"That how you'd do it?" Skip asked.

Carlyle gave him a look. "This pub is my pride and joy. I'd not go blowing bits off it for love nor money."

Skip smiled. "Yeah, but suppose it was a competitor's bar?"

"What do you take me for?"

"An old dog who knows all the tricks," Skip replied. He was working with his test kit while they talked.

"Well, it would depend what I was trying to accomplish," Carlyle said. "They could have blown the whole building, if they'd enough explosive. But it's a brick structure, very sturdy. It appears they were attempting to gain entry to my private apartment."

"Right. So, that how you'd do it?"

"Aye," Carlyle said thoughtfully, "were I expecting an armored door. If not, I'd merely bring a prybar and a sizable henchman."

"Right," Skip said again, but he was a little distracted. He muttered, "Thymol, sulfuric acid, ethyl alcohol... come on, you little bitch, tell me your secrets."

The detectives drew closer, waiting.

"Got it!" the bomb tech exclaimed, holding up his sample vial. The liquid had turned rose-colored. "C4."

"Can you tag it?" Webb asked. Government-issue explosives were chemically marked at manufacture, to make them easier to trace.

"Maybe," Skip said. "It's definitely military in origin. You don't make this shit in your bathtub."

Webb motioned Erin to the front door. She followed him outside, letting the bomb guys do their thing.

"O'Reilly, what were you doing here?" he asked once they were on the street and out of earshot of the folks inside.

"What do you mean?"

"You know damn well what I mean. This place gets hit with you in it? Okay, I'll buy that. Once. But twice? What's going on?"

"Nothing!" she said loudly. Then, lowering her voice, "I recognized the missing cases of whiskey. They were the same as the house brand here at the Corner. It's a really rare label. I thought maybe there was a connection. I was bracing Carlyle about it."

"Jones said you were talking to a CI," Webb said, speaking in a near-whisper. "Carlyle's middle management in the O'Malleys. Guys that high up in an organization don't spill to the cops. Not over chickenshit like this."

"He's been useful before," she said.

"All right. Who did this, then?"

"Hans Rüdel."

"Who the hell is Hans Rüdel?"

"A German mercenary."

"You know this from..." Webb said, cocking his head toward the Corner.

"Yeah."

"And you believe him?"

"Yeah, I do," Erin said. "We've got a guy in custody who speaks German. These are the guys who hit the *Loch Druich*."

"Is this a theory, or do you have proof?"

Erin almost snapped at the Lieutenant. She could feel her habitual defensiveness rising up in her, linking up with her residual adrenaline. Then she remembered what Kira had said. *Webb's a medium-large asshole sometimes, but you think he doesn't trust you? Erin, he's got you working point on your own case.* She took a deep breath and tried to calm herself.

"Something Carlyle said in there, just a minute ago. How guys would bring explosives, but only if they knew what they had to break through. He's right. Perps don't use breaching charges. They use crowbars and kick in doors. But Carlyle's door was steel-core. Bulletproof. They must've known what they had to deal with ahead of time."

Webb nodded. "There's wood paneling on the door," he said. "So they wouldn't have known just to look at it. Okay, I'll buy that they had inside info. But that doesn't prove a connection between the ship and this hit."

"There's the C4," she said. "And the Germans. And the whiskey. Sir, there's too much lining up for this to be coincidence."

"And they just happened to hit the place while you were there? Another coincidence?"

She shrugged. "Had to happen sometime."

He shook his head. "O'Reilly, you're gonna give me a heart attack." He took a drag on his cigarette and stared morosely into the Barley Corner's windows. "You want to watch out. You're gonna get yourself killed one of these days."

"And here I thought you didn't care," she said.

"I don't. But the paperwork would be a pain in the ass."

"Okay," Erin said. "So, we need to talk to the guy I tagged. I don't think he's hurt too bad. He should still be conscious and able to answer questions. We'll need someone who speaks German, and—"

"I'll handle it," Webb said. "You're off duty."

Erin was rendered momentarily speechless. "I'm... what?" she finally managed.

"You just shot a man," he said patiently. "You were standing right next to a bomb when it went off. And you got shot at. You are not coming back in to the office like nothing happened. You're turning in your gun to the Forensics guys, you're getting checked out by the EMTs, and then you're going home for the rest of the day."

"I'm fine," she protested.

"I don't care if you have three character witnesses, a note from your doctor, and an Old Testament prophet telling me you're fine." He looked her in the eye. "You can't possibly know that yet. You're still reacting. That happens to every officer in a situation like this. I wouldn't trust myself to think straight after a gunfight. This isn't about you. I know you're tough. Stop trying to prove it to me. Or to yourself."

*   *   *

In spite of Webb's instructions, Erin went to the vet before going home. Rolf didn't seem hurt, but he'd been standing pretty close to a sizable bomb and she didn't want to take chances. They sat in the veterinarian's waiting room for a quarter of an hour, Erin trying to read a magazine. She couldn't concentrate. Her eyes kept skipping words and she had to go back and reread the same sentences over and over.

She told herself she was fine, that worse things happened to cops all the time. She called herself weak, knew she should be stronger than this, but it didn't do any good.

An elderly white-haired woman moved into the seat next to hers. The woman had on an ancient floral-print dress and a pair of wire-rimmed spectacles. A gray cat with long, silky fur was resting in the crook of her arm. She reached out and patted the back of Erin's hand.

"There, there, dear," she said in a kindly voice. "Everything's going to be all right."

"Huh?" Erin flinched and stared at the other woman.

"I can see that you love him," the woman continued. "He's a beautiful dog, and so well behaved. I'm sure there's nothing to worry about. He looks very healthy."

"Oh. Uh, yeah," Erin said. "He is."

"You're trembling, dear. Don't you worry. Doctor Halverson is very good."

"I know," Erin said. She looked down at her hands. The old lady was right; she was shaking.

"What's the matter, dear?" the lady asked, peering at Rolf.

Rolf stared back. He didn't understand civilians.

"He got blown up," Erin said.

The old woman blinked through her glasses. "I'm sorry, dear. What was that?"

The receptionist saved her from an explanation. "Erin and Rolf? Next."

Rolf's prognosis was good. The vet said he might have some temporary hearing loss, but didn't think it was anything to worry about. The nosebleed was superficial.

"But take care not to have him near any explosions in the future," the vet said.

"Right," Erin said, trying not to roll her eyes. "Next time I'm planning to blow up a bomb, I'll leave him home."

* * *

Back at her apartment, Erin found herself at loose ends. A thousand things needed to be done, but she wasn't allowed to do them. She wanted to talk to Carlyle again. He knew something about the *Loch Druich* that he hadn't told her. He'd been the target of the same guys who'd whacked Garrity and Carr. That connected the O'Malleys to the ship, which meant...

Erin didn't know what it meant. But she knew it was important. And on top of that was the search for Janice Barnes's killer. Her squad was spread pretty thin. Why had Webb benched her? She was fine, damn it.

Except she wasn't. She was jumpy as hell. She couldn't think clearly. She kept wanting to reach for her gun. When she closed her eyes, she could still see the masked gunman coming around the corner.

Rolf was staring at her, head cocked to one side. She realized she'd been standing just inside her door for half a minute without moving.

"It's all right, boy," she said, wondering if she was telling the truth.

*   *   *

She decided to spend the rest of the day training Rolf. He needed several hours of it every week, and this way she felt like she was at least giving the NYPD some value for her salary. They practiced tracking and detection. His nosebleed didn't seem to have impaired his sense of smell. He went straight to every target as if he was following lit-up signs.

Working with him, Erin felt her equilibrium coming back. There was something about the K-9 that strengthened her. She remembered hearing that soldiers who handled military dogs had lower rates of PTSD than other veterans.

Her phone went off in her pocket. Pulling it out, she saw an unlisted number. She answered on the third ring.

"Hello?"

"Hello," said a quiet, polite man's voice. She thought she should recognize it, but didn't right away. "Is this Erin O'Reilly?"

"Who is this?"

"Trevor," he said. "Trevor Fairfax. We spoke earlier today."

Erin's memory caught up with her. "Yes, Mr. Fairfax. I'm Detective O'Reilly. Did you come up with something?"

There was a short pause. Then Trevor replied, "Not exactly, ma'am. But I've been thinking a great deal. About you."

"What do you mean?" she said sharply.

"Your face," he said. "I can still see you, as clearly as if you were standing in front of me. You're a very attractive woman, Erin."

"So?"

"I'd very much like to see you again," he said. "You're more than attractive. You're truly beautiful. I expect men tell you that all the time. But not everyone knows how to appreciate true beauty. You are extraordinary. I can't stop thinking about you."

"Mr. Fairfax," she said, "You just met me this morning. It's a little early for that sort of thing."

"I wouldn't want you to get the wrong idea," Trevor said quickly. "A lot of men, they only say a woman is attractive because they want to... to... well, you know. But I'm not like that."

"Mr. Fairfax," she said. "Thanks, but I'm not interested. It wouldn't be appropriate."

"I don't understand, Erin. I haven't said or done anything improper, I'm sure."

"That's not the point. I met you in the course of an investigation. I keep my work and personal life separate."

"With the long hours you work, you must lead a solitary life," Trevor said. His voice was warm, persuasive. "Even a lonely one. It's not like I'm your coworker, or an eyewitness, or a suspect. I'm just a man you met while you were shopping. I hope I didn't offend you in some way."

"No," she said. "But I'm not looking for a boyfriend right now."

There was an awkward pause.

"Maybe I'll see you again sometime," Trevor said, and he hung up.

Erin looked at her phone and wondered whether she ought to be having second thoughts. He wasn't a bad-looking guy, and he was polite. But she remembered her last relationship with a civilian. It hadn't ended well.

While she was staring at the phone, it buzzed in her hand, startling her so badly she almost dropped it. She expected to see an unknown number, Trevor calling back to try to change her mind. Instead, it was her sister-in-law.

"Hey, Shelly," Erin said.

"Hi, Erin," Michelle said. Her voice was flustered, distressed. "Look, I know you're busy, and it's an awful thing to spring something like this on short notice, but I need some help."

Erin's police experience flooded her imagination with a rich menu of possible catastrophes.

"What's the matter?" she asked sharply.

"I'm at Urgent Care with Patrick," the other woman said. "I'm sure it's nothing serious, but he's been throwing up all day. He just can't keep anything down. And now he's spiked a fever. And Sean's in surgery, and I couldn't get a sitter on short notice. I didn't want Anna here, and I was in such a hurry. I left her in front of the TV. Oh, God, I'm such a lousy mother—"

"Shelly, breathe," Erin interrupted. "Anna's a good kid, she'll be fine for a few minutes. I can be right there. Fifteen, twenty minutes, tops."

"Erin, you're a lifesaver," Michelle said, and Erin heard some of the tension fall away. "Anna's upset. You know how much she loves her kid brother. If you could do something to take her mind off it..."

"I'll take her to a movie," Erin suggested.

"Perfect! Thanks again, sis. I owe you."

*   *   *

Erin dropped Rolf inside and headed to Sean and Michelle's house. Sean O'Reilly Junior was her oldest brother and a trauma surgeon. Michelle was a sweet, kind woman who'd decided to be a stay-at-home mom. Her children, Anna and Patrick, were eight and six, respectively. Erin loved the whole family.

She tried not to worry about Patrick while she drove. Kids got the occasional bug. He'd be well cared for, and he'd probably be fine once they got some fluids in him. Her job was to take care of the other kid.

She had a spare key to the O'Reillys' brownstone. It was in an eye-wateringly expensive part of Midtown Manhattan. Sean Junior made five times Erin's salary, and it showed. Erin parked in a police space at the corner and jogged to the front door.

"Hey, Anna!" she called as she let herself in. "Where you at, kiddo?" Her question was immediately answered by the sound of the TV from the living room.

She made it a step and a half into the room before Anna wrapped herself around Erin's legs.

"How you doing, kiddo?" Erin asked.

"Mommy's at the hospital," Anna said in that super-serious voice only small children knew. "Patrick's going to have to have an IV and a saline drip."

Erin took a second to reflect on the unusual vocabulary a surgeon's kid developed. "Your mom thought you'd be bored here all by yourself," she said, keeping her voice light and cheerful. "And I was bored, too, so I thought I'd go to a movie. You want to come?"

"Can we see *Evil Dead*?"

Erin opened her mouth. Then she closed it again.

Anna giggled. "I'm just kidding, Auntie Erin. Mommy would ground me *forever*."

"She'd ground me, too," Erin laughed. "Tell you what. Anything that's G or PG."

"How about *Despicable Me 2*?"

"Works for me." Erin hadn't seen the first one, but didn't figure it'd matter.

"Where's Rolfie?"

"He doesn't go to movies."

"Why not?"

"Because he needs to rest so he can chase the bad guys tomorrow."

"Oh."

*   *   *

The movie was surprisingly enjoyable. Erin was more of a gritty action-flick fan, but it was a pleasure to step out of her own world for a little while. It was good to watch a movie with a kid every now and then, to keep from getting too jaded. Anna laughed and smiled and munched popcorn. Erin found herself wondering about having a kid of her own someday. Now there was a crazy thought, but it still made her smile, watching her niece. She put an arm around the girl's shoulder and let her snuggle in close.

Chapter 12

Erin woke up suddenly, sitting up in bed. She stared wildly into the darkness and groped for the light switch. She knocked the lamp over. Cursing, she fumbled on the floor. Rolf was on his feet beside her. She felt his snout against her shoulder.

She finally found the lamp and flicked it on. Her breathing slowly began to return to normal as the dream retreated. It'd been the same one she'd been having, all chaos and gunfire. She sat for a minute, one hand resting on Rolf's comforting bulk. The clock read 4:30. She got up and went into the bathroom.

Her eyes were dry and burning. Her neck, shoulders, and jaw ached. The face that stared back at her from the mirror looked like a ghost. Her interlude with her niece had been a nice break, but she was back in the grind.

She'd put Anna to bed and stayed at the house until her brother had come home, fresh from surgery and exhausted, at quarter to midnight. Patrick was going to be okay, of course, but Michelle was still at Urgent Care with him. Erin hadn't gotten to bed herself until almost twelve-thirty.

Four hours of unhealthy sleep would have to be enough. She had work to do. She drank two cups of coffee and gulped down some oatmeal. Then she put on her jogging clothes and took Rolf for their morning run. She already felt exhausted, but she pressed through it.

Eventually, she managed to find a little inner calm, listening to the thud of her shoes on the pavement, feeling her heartbeat. For a few minutes, everything else closed down.

Then the euphoria passed and she was back at her apartment, facing the same bullshit. She took a quick shower and went in to the precinct.

"Hey, O'Reilly," the duty sergeant called. Then he did a double take. "Whoa. You okay?"

"Fine," she said over her shoulder, on her way to the stairs.

"Must be that time of the month," she thought she heard him mutter. She ignored it. Some battles weren't worth fighting.

Webb was waiting for her up in Major Crimes. He had a cup of department-issue coffee in one hand and an unlit cigarette in the other.

"Morning, sir," she said.

"Morning," he said. "You've got a meeting downstairs."

"What about?"

"Departmental psych guy wants to talk to you."

"Oh, come on!" she snapped. "I just talked to him last month!"

"I know," Webb said.

"You're kidding."

"Do I look like I'm laughing? A Critical Incident is a Critical Incident. Stop pretending you don't know the protocol."

"Forget it, sir. I just want to get back to work."

"Then you should hurry down, because the sooner you talk to the doc, the sooner you'll be cleared for duty."

Erin swallowed her retort and stomped back down the stairs to the departmental psychiatrist's office, Rolf at her side. The door was open. She knocked on the doorframe.

"Come on in, Erin," the doctor said, standing up. "Could you get the door, please?"

She took two steps into the room, closed the door behind her, and stood at parade rest, hands clasped behind her back, staring straight ahead. Rolf sat beside her.

"Relax, Erin," he said, smiling. "This isn't an inspection."

"I thought that's exactly what it is," she said without moving.

"Okay, have it your way, Soldier," he said, sitting on the front edge of his desk. She glanced at him for a second, then went back to looking at his wall.

Doctor Evans was a few years older than Erin. His hair was going a thin and gray. He had a very ordinary face for a psychiatrist, with the exception of a fearsome scar that ran the whole length of his left cheek. No one knew how he'd gotten it, though of course there were all kinds of stories.

He really wasn't a bad guy. Erin even liked him. But she didn't like what he represented. She didn't like anyone telling her what she could or couldn't do.

"I understand you swapped bullets again yesterday," Evans said.

"Yes, sir."

"You want to talk about it?"

"Does it matter?"

"Do you want to get better?"

"I'm fine."

"We're not machines, Erin," he said, taking off his glasses and wiping them with a pocket handkerchief. "We're living creatures."

Erin didn't say anything.

"Machines that break down can't fix themselves," Evans went on. "But people aren't like that. We're in a constant state of growth and decay, life and death competing in us. Some parts of us are growing, even as other parts are dying. You know what I mean?"

"I guess so."

"When something bad happens, parts of us wither. It's my job to make sure the whole works don't shut down."

"I'm not broken, sir."

"No, you're not," he said. "Not yet."

She looked at him head-on. "I'm not going to break," she said. "No matter what."

"Are you wanting me to tell you you're strong?" Evans said. "Why? Do you need someone else to tell you that?"

Erin blinked. That wasn't what she'd meant. Was it?

"I'm going to ask you a couple of questions," he said. "I just have one rule. You're not allowed to answer them 'fine' or 'okay.' Can you do that?"

"Yeah."

"How are you sleeping?"

The first two words that wanted to come out of her mouth were the ones she wasn't allowed to say. She hesitated. She was honest, but she wasn't a whiner.

Evans waited.

"I wake up still tired," she said at last.

"Do you know why?"

"Sometimes I... have dreams." It was hard to say it.

"What sort of dreams?"

"Like instant replay. Stuff that happened."

"The gunfight at the airport?"

"Yeah."

"The shootout in Brighton Beach?"

"That, too."

"Do you know why you wake up tired?" he asked again.

She shook her head.

"Our subconscious is there to help us," Evans said. "We're

social animals. We're built to deal with things by communicating with other people. We're so focused on that, it's like we have a built-in conversation partner in our own heads. The problem is, if we don't talk to other people about things that bother us, we end up having the whole conversation with ourselves. You're trying to work through something tough, Erin, and you're doing all the work yourself. You don't need to talk to me."

"Like hell I don't. My CO ordered me down here."

Evans laughed. "I have to sign a form that says we've talked and you're cleared for duty," he said. "The form says I've evaluated your mental and emotional health. But you don't have to say a word to me about what's really on your mind, not if you don't want to."

Erin looked at him, not knowing what to say.

"But you do need someone," he said. "Some people find it easiest to talk to a mental health professional. Others have a close friend, a family member. You have someone like that?"

Erin thought of Kira and their lunch the day before. Then, for some crazy reason, she thought of Carlyle. "I don't know," she said.

"Your father's a retired officer, isn't he?"

"Yeah." Of course he'd seen that in her personnel file.

"Would he be a good person for you to talk with?"

Erin snorted. "He never even fired his gun on the job."

"Most officers don't," Evans said.

"So I'm special, huh?"

"Do you feel special?"

"I feel like shit."

The words hung there in the office. Erin wished she could suck them back into her mouth.

"Why do you say that?"

"There's a gang of hitmen running around New York right

now," she said. "They've killed four people we know of. And there's another guy who's knocking off women in hotel rooms."

"A serial killer?" Evans asked, looking closely at her.

She wasn't supposed to say so, but at this point she didn't really care what Webb said. "Yeah."

"Does that bother you?"

"Of course it does!"

"I mean, does it bother you particularly?"

"Why should it?"

One corner of Evans's mouth curled up. "It's not very politically correct of me to bring this up," he said. "But you are a woman."

"You noticed."

"It would be natural to feel more empathy with a female victim," he said. "You know this, of course. Just like I know you're a woman in a job that's two-thirds male, and dominated by masculine traditions and what I think you probably refer to as 'macho bullshit.'"

Erin couldn't help smiling a little at that. "What about it?"

"You probably feel some pretty intense pressure to measure up. To be more manly than the men."

"That's not always hard to do."

"That's exactly the sort of mindset I mean," Evans said, nodding. "When you're on the job, you feel like you have to clamp down pretty hard on anything you think of as weak, soft, or feminine."

"Feminine doesn't mean weak!" she retorted.

Evans raised an eyebrow. "Of course it doesn't," he said. "But it's a part of you that you keep locked down in your subconscious, along with your shooting trauma. The more baggage you cram in there, the more crowded it's going to get. The subconscious can be a real pressure cooker, Erin. I'd like to see you let off some of that steam safely."

She could see his point. But she could also see just enough of herself to know that if she let some of those feelings out, she might totally lose it. She had to keep her shit together. "I'll think it over," she said.

"That's what people say when they're planning not to think about something, if they can help it," Evans sighed. "Don't worry, I'll sign your form. Congratulations, Detective. You're cleared for duty."

"That's it?" Erin blurted out. The way he'd been talking, she'd expected him to press harder.

"Half the officers in the NYPD are closer to the edge than you are," he said. "It's a stressful job. Why do you think the city pays my salary? Go on, take your dog and dive back in. But drop me a line when you do decide you're ready to talk."

"Copy that."

"I'm glad you've got your partner there," he said, indicating Rolf with a tilt of his chin. "Dogs are good helpers for this sort of thing."

"I don't need a psych degree to tell me that," she said.

* * *

"Welcome back," Vic said when Erin and Rolf walked onto the second floor. "What's the verdict?"

"Turns out I'm not crazy."

"I should've gone with you," he said. "I could've told him that wasn't true."

"Asshole."

"Psycho."

"Get a room, you two," Kira said. "Take care of some of that tension and come back when you're ready to work."

Webb ignored her and looked at Erin. "You good to go?"

"Yeah," she said. "What'd I miss?"

He sighed. "The guy we've got in custody won't say anything. Not word one. He hasn't even asked for a lawyer."

"I think he only speaks German," Erin said.

Webb shrugged. "Doesn't matter. He's got no ID on him, we don't have his prints on file. You think he could be this Rüdel guy Carlyle mentioned to you?"

It was Erin's turn to shrug. "Beats me. From what Carlyle said, it sounded like he didn't know him personally, just by reputation."

"Any idea why Rüdel would be gunning for Carlyle?"

"Taking over the O'Malleys, maybe?" she guessed. But even as she said it, it didn't sound quite right to her.

"Or just taking out Carlyle," Kira said. "A guy in his line of work makes a lot of enemies."

"Rüdel's a contractor, going by what Carlyle told me," Erin said. "That means he's working for somebody."

"Carlyle won't say who," Vic said.

"Did you ask him?" Erin asked.

Vic snorted. "He's a mob guy. Yeah, he's just aching to spill his guts and tell all his secrets to the NYPD. Why the hell didn't I think of that?"

"Anyway, that's not our only problem," Webb said. "Holliday called me a couple minutes ago, gave me a heads-up."

"What'd the Captain want?" Erin asked.

"He's letting us know the Feebies are nosing around," Webb said. "Homeland Security, too."

"Shit," Vic muttered. "Goddamn Feds."

"What for?" Erin asked.

"They're saying it's potentially international," Webb explained. "If this Rüdel is a German national, and if the Scottish guys were killed in international waters, then it's a federal case."

"No way were they killed that far offshore," Kira said. "I

checked the tide charts. The bodies were dumped close in."

"Whatever," Webb said. "The Captain's handling the Feds for the moment, but there's a lot of pressure. Plus, with the explosives, Homeland Security is considering calling these guys terrorists."

"This was an attempted murder," Erin said. "Not terrorism."

"This was actual murder, O'Reilly," Webb corrected her. "Four of them, in fact."

She shook her head. "Those were incidental. Carlyle was the target. The others were just in the way."

"Bodyguards," Vic said.

"You think the killers knew about them?" Kira asked.

"Absolutely," Vic said. "You saw the bullet pattern in their booth. One of them didn't even have the chance to get up. These guys came in and gunned them down right on the spot. Tierney, the waitress, said they didn't even say anything, they just started shooting. And they didn't bother to come behind the bar and shoot her or the bartender."

"They weren't trying to eliminate witnesses," Erin said, understanding.

Vic nodded. "Which tells us nothing."

"It tells us the same thing the breaching charge does," Erin said. "The hitmen had inside information about the Barley Corner and Carlyle's defensive measures."

"Which they probably got from torturing the guys on the boat," Webb said. "And of course that's where they got the C4. Taylor and the Bomb Squad ran the chemical markers on the explosive residue."

"It's British military issue," Kira said. "Probably from a batch that went missing from Walcheren Barracks in Glasgow last month."

"I called the Brits to verify," Vic said. "They'll get back to us. Sometime."

"Stolen, or sold by corrupt soldiers?" Erin asked.

"This is the British army we're talking about," Webb said. "These guys don't sell their weapons for extra cash. What do you think they are, the Russians?"

"I resent that!" Vic said.

"Am I wrong?" Webb retorted.

Vic silently fumed.

"The Glasgow connection strongly suggests this was a smuggling operation the *Loch Druich* was involved in," Webb went on. "I'm guessing we'll find out Smiling Jack is an arms dealer. It's a safe assumption that Garrity and Carr were working for him, helping transport the C4 to the States."

"What for?" Erin asked.

"Resale, probably," Kira said. "Unless you can think of a reason the O'Malleys would want a few kilos of military-grade explosives."

"Kilos?" Erin echoed. "They didn't use that much to blow the door at the Corner."

"Then the rest of it's still out there," Webb said. "Happy thought."

"So, the guy we've got," Erin said. "We don't even have a name?"

"I said that," Webb said. "No prints, no facial recognition, nothing."

"Interpol?" she suggested.

Vic smiled humorlessly. "I called them and sent the prints over. I asked about Rüdel too. They're checking."

"What about tracking Rüdel?" Erin asked. "Assuming he's not the guy we've got now."

"We'll put out a BOLO," Webb said. "For a guy in a mask with a German accent."

"Right," Erin said, feeling a little foolish. "Never mind."

"We're going to have to wait until we hear back from our

friends in Europe," Webb said. "In the meantime, we have to work the O'Malley angle. Find the motive, we may find who's behind this. You want to take another run at Carlyle?" he asked Erin.

"Sure," she said. She wanted to talk to him very much. She had the feeling he knew something important. "Where is he?"

"He wasn't hurt badly enough to be hospitalized," Webb said. "And he's technically a victim, so he's not under arrest. We asked for contact info, and he said he'd be staying at a friend's place while the Corner gets repaired." The Lieutenant checked his case notes. "Looks like he's staying with James Corcoran."

"This keeps getting better," Erin said under her breath.

"Is there a problem?" Webb asked.

"Nothing I can't handle, sir."

"Apparently, he also passed along word that he wouldn't mind seeing you in person, to thank you for your assist."

"Great," Erin said, putting as much sarcasm into one word as she could.

* * *

After her abortive fling with James Corcoran had come to an end, Erin had assumed she'd never see the inside of Corky's home. Now the circumstances were a little weird, to put it mildly. But Erin had told Webb she could handle it, and she was determined to do just that.

Corky's address was Midtown Manhattan, in a ludicrously overpriced high-rise. Crime, apparently, paid some people just fine. Erin flashed her shield to the doorman, who opened the door for her and Rolf without comment. In the lobby were three tough-looking young men. In spite of the warm weather, the three guys were all wearing bulky jackets. Erin wondered what she'd find if she did a stop-and-frisk on them. Probably enough weaponry to take over Panama. But she wasn't a Patrol officer anymore, and besides, stop-and-frisk was on its way out. Too much political fallout and too many innocents getting targeted. Erin settled for giving them a hard stare as she passed them. They replied with similar stares. One of them gave a slight nod that hinted at respect. Behind her, she saw the doorman sending a text on his phone. Clearly, she was expected.

The elevator took her all the way to the top. The doors opened to reveal two more bulky guys, one with a Celtic neck tattoo. There was a tense, silent moment.

"NYPD," she said, cocking her hip to show her shield where it was clipped to her belt.

"Detective," the guy on the left said, giving an appreciative look both to the shield and the hip it rested on. Both of them watched her all the way down the hallway to Corky's door.

She rapped on the door with her knuckles. Almost before the sound died away, it swung open.

"Erin, love," Corky said. "I'd been wondering when I might find you standing in my doorway." He was smiling that boyish, irresistible smile of his, with a bright sparkle in his green eyes.

"Hi, Corky," she said. "I heard you were hiding Cars. You got him in there somewhere?"

"Why don't you have a look?" he said. "You can search as thoroughly as you like." But he made no move to get out of the way.

"Corky," Carlyle's voice came from inside. "Don't you find it a mite rude to keep a lady waiting on the doorstep?"

"I've been called a great many things," Corky said, "but rarely rude." He stepped to the side and spread one arm in welcome. "Do come in, love."

Erin stepped into the apartment, instinctively checking the corners. She was surprised by how ordinary the place looked on the inside. She'd been in a Midtown apartment before, on an earlier case, and it had been full of priceless artwork and antiques. Corky's suite was very middle-class, even blue-collar. He had posters of soccer players on the walls, a couple pinups of female athletes, and a framed photo of the New York Yankees that looked to have been signed by the whole team. The furniture was in good repair and looked comfortable, but was nothing special.

"You bring your girlfriends here?" she couldn't help asking.

"Oh no, love," he said brightly. "I take them to my other place."

Carlyle was standing in the living room, a glass of whiskey in one hand. He'd gotten a change of clothes and was every inch the dapper gentleman. It struck her, not for the first time, how different these two Irishmen were from one another. "Erin," he said. "I knew they'd send someone to talk to me soon, but I admit I wasn't expecting you."

"Why not?"

"Now who's being rude?" Corky said. "The lass is standing here without a drink in her hand, and you're talking at her. What's your pleasure, love?"

"I don't need anything."

"I didn't ask what you needed. I asked what would pleasure you."

She gave Corky a slow once-over and let him see her do it. Then she shook her head. "Can't see anything that would."

Carlyle chuckled. Corky laughed out loud.

"You're an Irish lass," Corky said. "I'll go out on a limb and pour you a whiskey." He went to a side table and got a bottle of—what else—Glen D. "Soda? Rocks? Straight up?"

"Ice," she said, giving up. It was a hot day, and holding something cold in her hand wouldn't be such a bad thing.

Corky dropped two ice cubes into a glass and poured a double Scotch over them. Then he made a second drink, handed her one, and kept the other for himself.

"Perhaps we should sit down," Carlyle suggested.

"Okay." Erin took a seat in an armchair. Carlyle took the other armchair in the room. Corky sprawled out on the couch against the wall. Rolf sat next to Erin's chair.

"So," Corky said. "Thank you for coming to see me, Erin. I know you're a busy lass, and it means the world to me."

Erin and Carlyle looked at him.

He grinned. "Well, a lad can dream. I know you've come to see Cars. After all, you hadn't time to complete your business at your prior meeting. Come to that, what exactly was that business?"

"I think maybe this should be a private conversation," Erin said to Carlyle.

"In our fine legal system, a lad's permitted to retain counsel, I believe," Carlyle said.

"You telling me he's your lawyer?" Erin said in disbelief.

"The word I used was 'counsel,'" Carlyle said. "There's no one I trust more, this side of the pond."

"That's not to say he trusts me," Corky put in. "Be careful what you infer from this lad, Erin. He's practically a lawyer himself. But we're best mates, and that counts for a lot."

"Have it your way," Erin said. "But we need to talk about what happened."

"I couldn't agree more," Carlyle said.

"So let's start talking," she said. "Who are Daniel Carr and Sean Garrity?"

"Murder victims, as I understand it," Carlyle said.

"You knew them," she said. "Did they work for you?"

"I have three bartenders, two of them part-time, a cook, two kitchen assistants, and four waitresses on my payroll."

"Did these guys make deliveries to you?"

"I don't keep the names of all the lads who deliver food and drink to the Corner."

"But they knew about the reinforced door to your apartment."

Carlyle paused. "No," he said after a moment. "I don't imagine they would have known a thing like that."

"Erin," Corky broke in. "You're surely not suggesting those poor bastards had anything to do with the unpleasantness at the pub."

She glanced at him. "Are you?"

"Erin suspects they were slain by the same men who attacked the Corner," Carlyle said. "She's attempting to build a connection. I'm sure she's not implying those lads were involved in anything improper with me or mine."

"They were smuggling explosives," Erin said. "Some of which were then used to blow down your door. Explosives procured by an arms dealer called Smiling Jack."

Carlyle sipped his whiskey and said nothing.

"Rüdel is running around New York killing people," she said. "*Your* people, Cars. We're on the same team, for Christ's sake. Don't you want him to be found?"

"Aye," Carlyle said. "I do."

"Then help me!"

"Erin," he said gently. "Who am I?"

"What do you mean?"

"It's a simple question. Look at me. Who am I?"

She didn't like this sort of game. Looking him in the eye, she gave it to him straight. "You're Morton Carlyle. Irish immigrant. Former IRA terrorist. Expert bomb-maker. Gambling bookie. Mid-level O'Malley associate. And owner of the Barley Corner pub."

"Do you think I'm what you call a civilian? Do you believe I pick up the telephone and dial 911 when something goes amiss?"

Corky tried not to laugh and almost succeeded. He turned it

into a cough.

"You know what?" Erin said. "I don't understand you, not one bit. You're in danger. People tried to kill you in your own home, I saved your ass, and you still won't let me help."

Corky was still grinning, but Carlyle wasn't. "A lad like me is always in danger," he said. "You think I have the luxury of choosing a safe path? Or have you ever thought that trying to avoid one danger might put me square in the path of another?"

"You're worried about your own people," she said.

"If you were to start associating with known criminals, who would you have to fear?" Carlyle asked. "Your new associates, or your fellow officers? Or both?"

"That's not the same thing," she said.

He didn't bother to argue the point.

"Anyway," she said, "Rüdel's a menace."

"I agree," Carlyle said. "Anyone who takes him off the street will be doing the world a favor."

"And you're all about the favors," she said.

"I am," he agreed. "And I'll not forget you've saved my life. Again."

"I trusted you," she said. "I put a gun in your hand."

"You can still trust me," he said softly. "I'm no enemy, Erin. And I'd like to be your friend."

"In exchange for what?" She hadn't really meant to say it. The words just popped out.

"This isn't a business transaction," he said.

"Okay. What can you tell me, then? As a friend?"

"I can tell you anything that doesn't infringe on my own business, nor that of my associates."

"What's that got to do with Rüdel?" she asked.

"Nothing. As I told you, he's merely a facilitator. He's not doing this for himself, save for a paycheck."

"So who's writing his checks?"

"I can't possibly answer that."

"Can't, or won't?"

"Is the distinction important?"

"I'd say it is," Corky interjected. "For instance, if a lass says she'll not sleep with a lad, if she means she won't, she's still persuadable. If she means she *can't*, well..."

"Corky," Carlyle said, "must you view every philosophical question through the same lens?"

"These are the eyes the good Lord gave me," he said cheerfully.

"Cars," Erin said, ignoring Corky, "do you know who hired Rüdel to come after you?"

"No."

The flat denial startled her. She'd been expecting another dodge. But as she thought about it, she realized why. He'd had no problem answering the exact question she'd asked. She tried again.

"Who do you think hired Rüdel? In your opinion?"

"I couldn't say."

And just like that, they were back on philosophical grounds.

Erin stood up. She put her drink down, untouched. "Sorry to waste your time. And mine."

Carlyle rose politely. "I'm sorry you feel that way."

Something in the way he said it caught her attention. He actually did look sorry. But he had such good self-control, she wasn't sure it wasn't an act. "See you around, Cars. Corky."

Corky snatched up her discarded drink. "Drop by any time, love."

Her phone buzzed in her pocket, saving her from any more back-and-forth. She nodded to the two men and led Rolf out, putting the phone to her ear as she exited the apartment.

"O'Reilly," she said.

"This is Levine."

"Hey," Erin said. "What'd you find out?" She nodded to the Irish thugs by the elevator, got on, and pushed the button for the ground floor.

"Negative on the lipstick," Levine said. "It wasn't possible to tell how much time elapsed since application."

For a second, Erin couldn't remember what she was talking about. Then she shifted gears back to her other case. "Okay, it was a thought," she said. But she knew the ME wouldn't be calling just to report a negative test result. "What else have you got?"

"The victim was drugged twice."

"Say what?"

"The wine bottle tested positive for Rohypnol, but not for cyanide."

"But she was killed by cyanide, right?"

"Tox screen shows lethal levels," Levine confirmed. "I'm confident cyanide poisoning was cause of death. But there was no quantity of cyanide in the victim's stomach. It appears the agent was not orally administered."

Erin leaned against the back of the elevator. "So, what's that mean? Needle stick?"

"There's no trace of gas in the lungs, so the agent was almost certainly introduced into the bloodstream."

"What are you telling me? The killer drugged her, then gave her a shot?"

"That's correct," Levine said. "Judging from the amount of Rohypnol in her blood, she had probably been unconscious for some time, at least half an hour, before death."

"And there was no sign of sexual assault?"

"None."

The elevator reached the lobby. Erin walked out past the second batch of goons. She tried to think. "Any idea where the needle strike was?"

"I'll check," Levine said. "It wouldn't have bled much, if at all, and there are a lot of places you can put a needle without leaving obvious signs."

Erin loaded Rolf into her car and got behind the wheel of the Charger. She cocked her head against her shoulder to hold the phone while she buckled up and started the engine. "Okay, I'm coming back to the precinct now. Are you done with your report?"

"I'll send it up," Levine said. "One other thing. The victim's clothing was changed antemortem."

"He dressed her up before killing her? I thought it was after."

"I told you what I meant."

"How can you tell?"

"There was a ripped seam in the dress. Even though she was drugged, she would have convulsed as the cyanide took effect."

Erin tried not to imagine the scene and failed. She suppressed a shudder. "The clothing tore when she thrashed around."

"Correct. Then she was posed in a resting posture."

"Anything else?"

"No." And Levine hung up.

Chapter 13

"Any luck?" Vic asked.

"What do you think?" Erin snapped. She glared at the whiteboard in the Major Crimes office. "It's a goddamn game to these guys, even when they nearly get killed."

"I didn't think he'd spill anything," Webb said. "But it was worth a try."

"We still don't even have an ID on the wounded guy," Kira said. "Interpol hasn't gotten back to Vic yet."

"So we're stalled," Erin said.

"Oh, one thing," Webb said. "We got the ballistics report from CSU from the Barley Corner shooting. It's funny. They said the guy we've got in custody was shot with two different guns."

"Yeah, those were mine," she said. "My Glock and my backup piece."

"Holy shit," Vic said. "Guns in both hands. Shootout at the O.K. Corral."

"No," Erin sighed. "Carlyle had my backup."

The others stared at her. There was an awkward silence.

"You gave *him* one of your guns?" Kira finally said.

"He didn't have his own?" Vic asked at almost the same moment.

"He doesn't carry," Erin said.

"That's the craziest thing I've heard this week," Webb said. "And that's saying something."

"I bet he goes strapped after this," Vic said.

"Whatever," Erin said. "It'll be in my report. I loaned him the gun, it was clear self-defense. What's it matter?"

Webb shook his head, a hint of a smile on his face. "It's a little unusual," he said.

Kira wasn't smiling. "You know the provisions of SAFE, right?"

Erin did. The Secure Ammunition and Firearms Enforcement Act had just gone into effect. It was a tough gun-control law with several provisions dictating sale and transfer of guns. "That doesn't apply here," she said.

"If he's prohibited from owning a gun, that's criminal facilitation," Kira said. "On you, Erin."

"Jesus," Vic said. "Once Internal Affairs, always Internal Affairs. That's a load of bullshit and you know it. You gonna lock her up, or what?"

"Carlyle's allowed to own a gun," Erin said. "He was never convicted of a felony, or even charged with one, at least not in this country."

"He's a terrorist!" Vic said.

"Whose side are you on here, Neshenko?" Webb wondered. "Just so I can keep things straight."

Vic threw his hands in the air. "I don't know! These guys are all assholes. Can't we just arrest all of them?"

"As far as I can tell, Carlyle didn't do anything," Erin shot back. "Except try not to die when his bar got shot up."

"Whose side are *you* on?" Vic retorted.

"The law's," she said. "Is there something you want to charge him with? Because being an asshole isn't illegal in New York, last time I checked."

"Thank God for that," Webb said. "Otherwise we'd be out of space in lockup pretty quick. And I'd have to arrest half the people in this room, to start with."

"What's that supposed to mean?" Vic snapped.

"It means that's enough, God damn it!" Webb shouted.

An angry, embarrassed silence followed.

"Okay," the Lieutenant said, more calmly. "I get it. We're all upset. But we've got a case to close and a killer to catch."

"Two killers," Erin said.

"The bartender said there were three," Kira said. "We caught one, so that still leaves two."

"That's not what I meant," Erin said. "I was talking about the hotel case."

"Give it a rest, Erin," Vic said. "We need to nail this one down first."

"Okay," she said. "How do we find Rüdel? Tell me."

More silence.

"Do you have a lead on the Barnes case?" Webb asked her.

"I might," Erin said, exaggerating.

"Okay, fine," Webb said. "It might be better if you step away from this one for a little while anyway. Find what you can on the hotel and run with it. The rest of us will keep working the Irish angle, see what we can get. And Neshenko?"

"Yeah?" Vic was still angry.

"Before you say the next insubordinate thing that pops into your head, imagine my size twelve walking shoe, and think about how far up your ass I can put it."

Vic actually smiled. "Careful, sir. Keep talking dirty to me, I can't be responsible for the consequences."

* * *

Erin really didn't have much in the way of leads. She knew the killer had drugged Janice Barnes, dressed her up, and poisoned her. She knew the brand of perfume he'd put on his victim. She knew he'd watched Janice die, then eased his way out of the hotel room, worked the chain lock from outside, and left it locked.

That meant he'd been in the room at least twice, maybe three times. Once to fix the chain so he could open and close it from outside, the second time to drug her, and the third to finish the murder.

Which told her nothing.

She rubbed her temples and tried to think. A big part of her was still wrapped up in the shootout at the Corner. Maybe Doc Evans should've kept her off the street a while longer.

There was one thing she could think of. She'd been wondering about it ever since she'd had the idea she might be tracking a serial killer. She started scanning the case files for unsolved locked-room killings.

There weren't any open cases that fit the MO.

That didn't necessarily mean anything. Her own squad had initially thought Janice might be a suicide. She ran a search in the CompStat system asking for suicides over the past three years. The computer gave her the phone book, of course. She noted that the rate was increasing year by year, which reinforced her dad's opinion that the world was gradually going to hell. There'd been 503 three years ago, 509 two years back, 557 the last year, and an even 300 in just the first half of the current one. Way too many to sort through.

Serial killers were pretty consistent. If this guy had killed a woman once, that was probably his thing. She eliminated men from her search, which left her with only 129, 128, and 163 for the past three years.

Still too many.

She kept working it down. Only fifteen percent of suicides were white women. About eight percent were between eighteen and twenty-five years old. That was a tiny proportion of the total.

Erin got up for a cup of coffee. A box of donuts in the break room still had a cruller, slightly stale. She took that, too, and went back to her desk. She gave Rolf half the cruller. He enjoyed his half more than she did hers.

She started pulling up individual files, looking for patterns. Almost immediately, she scored. A young woman back in 2011 had died at the DoubleTree and had been classified a suicide. Erin read the report. All the details fit. Locked room, no sign of a struggle, cyanide poisoning. The girl, Monica Albright, age twenty-one, had been a Junior at NYU. And she'd been found in a black dress with a bouquet of red roses.

"Lieutenant!" she called.

Webb strolled over. "You know, you took the last donut," he said. "That means you're buying the next box."

So that was why the cruller had still been there, damn it. "Take a look at this, sir," she said, pointing to her computer screen.

He leaned over her shoulder and read the file. When he'd finished, he stood back and closed his eyes.

"Well?" she prompted after giving him a minute.

Webb pinched the bridge of his nose. "What do you want me to say? That you were right? Okay, you're right. It's a series. This was, what, two years back?"

"Yeah," she said. "I haven't finished checking the records, though. There may have been others since then."

"And this one was declared a suicide," he said. "Just great. We're supposed to clear murder cases, not dig up cold ones."

"So, you want me to put it back?"

"Of course not," he sighed. "Does this help us?"

She shrugged. "It means the killer's using this hotel."

"Yeah," Webb said, nodding. "Current employee?"

"Or former. Is this enough for a court order for employment records?"

"I'll take it to Judge Ferris," Webb said. "He's good for this kind of thing. I'll get you the order by the end of the day, assuming he's awake."

"Awake?"

"Ferris is seventy-eight," Webb explained. "He usually takes an afternoon nap. But he's a good man. You need anything else?"

"I'll let you know, sir."

"Good work, O'Reilly." Webb went back to his own desk.

She was just getting back to checking the records when her phone buzzed.

"Yeah?" she said absentmindedly.

"Erin?"

His voice might not have been the one she least wanted to hear at the moment, but it was probably in the bottom ten. "Mr. Carlyle," she said flatly.

"Aye," Carlyle said. "I hope I've not interrupted anything."

"What do you want?"

"I'd like to assist you."

"News to me."

"I understand you're a trifle upset, Erin," he said. "But I've something you may want to hear."

Her jaw was clenched. She took a deep breath and tried to loosen up a little. "Keep talking."

"One of my lads just told me something interesting. It seems you've acquired an admirer."

"If this is about Corky..." she began.

"That's not what I mean," he said. "When you left the apartment, a lad across the street was photographing you."

Just what she needed. "Goddamn reporters," she muttered.

"I'm thinking not," Carlyle said. "My lad's canny. I trust his instincts, and he told me this man was attempting not to be seen."

"But your guy noticed him anyway?" Erin asked. "He trained in counter-surveillance, or what?"

"He was trained as a scout sniper by the Marine Corps," Carlyle replied coolly. "He's a fair eye for people out of place."

"Jesus," she said. "What do you need a guy like that for?"

"Security," Carlyle said, and she could hear the sardonic smile even over the phone. "If he says this lad's no reporter, I believe him."

"Why are you telling me this?"

"I want to give you all the help I can."

"In exchange for what?" she demanded.

"I told you before," he said. "We're not performing business transactions. I don't do business with coppers."

"Yeah, you're all heart. What's your game, Cars?"

"The same one you're playing, darling," he said. "I've no doubt you'll see your way to the end of this round. When you do, we'll talk again."

"Don't hold your breath," she said and hung up.

*   *   *

Judge Ferris had been awake. It took Webb less than an hour to get the court order in hand. By that time, Erin had a list of three more suspicious hotel-room deaths that had been classified as suicides. She also had a serious case of the creeps.

"One more at the DoubleTree," she said to Webb. "Last year. Same MO. Nicole Winslow, twenty-one. And two at motels, a Super 8 and a Motel 6, both near the Jersey border. Those are four years old."

"You sure about all of them?" Webb asked.

She shrugged. "Hard to be sure. The ones here in Manhattan, absolutely. The other two are sloppier. The first one was partially nude."

"Strange," Webb muttered, looking over her shoulder at the file on her computer. "A killer who evolves to give his victims more clothes? Typically they escalate to more violence, not less."

"I think he was figuring out what he likes," she said. "If he gets a sexual thrill out of it, maybe it took the first time or two to learn it wasn't about seeing the women naked."

Webb nodded. "That's not the point for this guy," he said. "It's the killing that gets him off."

"Not quite," Erin said. She'd been staring at the photos from all of the scenes. "It's the act of watching them die. It's pretty impersonal, right? How do most serial killers do it?"

"Strangulation. Blades. Blunt-force trauma."

"Right," she said. "But this guy uses poison. He drugs them, dresses them up, injects them, and sits back to watch them die."

"You think he films them?" Webb suggested.

"He could," she said. "Yeah, probably. That'll help us when we catch him. He'll have the film. Should be a slam-dunk."

"But he's not going to stop until we run him down," Webb said. "He knows what he wants now. These last three, they're all the same. He's got the taste for it."

Erin stood up and took the court order. "Rolf and I are going to the hotel," she said.

"Let me know if you need anything," he said. "We have to keep looking for Rüdel, but I want to nail this son of a bitch as bad as you do. It won't be long before he finds another victim."

Chapter 14

The hotel manager wasn't happy to see Erin again. She knew why. A guest who committed suicide was an embarrassment and could be bad for business. A murdered guest was much worse. No hotel liked having police detectives wandering around in any case. It made the guests edgy.

The court order permitted Erin to access guest and employee lists and to search the premises, though not to search any occupied room without the current occupant's permission. She'd need a warrant specifying any guest she needed to search. Unless the management evicted the guest, in which case the hotel could give her the necessary permission. The Fourth Amendment sometimes made her head hurt.

She wasn't expecting the killer to still be at the hotel, though. The guest list was the main thing, combined with one other idea she'd had. In her pocket was her bottle of Heartbreaker perfume.

The manager accompanied her to the fourteenth floor. He chattered nervously the whole way up. Erin didn't really listen. When the elevator doors slid open, she went straight to Room 1410.

"Could you take the tape down soon?" the manager pleaded. "It spoils the aesthetic of the hallway terribly. Our guests expect to feel secure, safe, not as if they're staying in... in..." He couldn't finish the sentence.

"We'll have it taken down as soon as the CSU guys are done," she said over her shoulder. "Shouldn't be long."

"Good, good," he said. "It's not that I don't appreciate what you're doing here. This whole thing is awful, awful. Such a terrible accident."

She stopped and turned to face him. "This wasn't an accident."

"Oh, yes, of course," he stammered. "A tragedy, I should have said." He handed her the passkey.

"Stay in the hallway, please," she said. The real tragedy for the manager was the bad publicity, Erin thought sourly. 1410 had already been gone over pretty thoroughly by the techies. They'd taken the bedding, the wine bottle, the glassware, even cut out the section of carpet the wine had spilled on. She stood in the middle of the room and thought things over, trying to reconstruct the crime.

The killer rented the room, using fake ID. Janice Barnes came up, either alone or with him. She opened the bottle of wine and had a drink. When the drug took effect, she fell over and spilled what was left of her drink. The killer clothed her in the black dress and injected her with cyanide. She died without ever regaining consciousness. Then he put the bouquet of roses in her hands, posed her, and left, taking Janice's own clothes with him. No, he tidied up a little before he left. A fastidious pyschopath. The wine glass had been put back on the table next to the bottle. A single glass, which suggested Janice had been drinking alone.

Erin kept coming back to the wine. It was the house label, with the DoubleTree's logo. She turned to the manager, who was fidgeting just outside the door. "Sir," she said. "Do you keep records of room service calls?"

"Naturally. They're billed to customers at checkout."

"Was there an order from this room?"

"I don't think so. I'd have to check."

"Would you, please?" she asked, managing to only grit her teeth a little.

He used his cell phone to call down to the hotel's billing agent. "No, ma'am," he said after a short conversation. "There were no additional charges. No pay-per-view either."

"Do an inventory of your wine stock," Erin said. "You're going to find a bottle missing."

"Ma'am, if you're suggesting one of our employees is pilfering our stores, you will find yourself quite mistaken," he said, his nervousness giving way to indignation.

"I'm suggesting someone stole one of your bottles and took it to this room," she said. "While you're at it, see if anything else is missing."

The manager glared at her. She glared right back, and after a few moments, he coughed and looked away. He made another call on his cell. "Herbert? Yes, I need to know of any inventory discrepancies. Of any sort, but particularly the wine stock. Yes, I understand. Thank you." He hung up and looked back at Erin. "It will take some time. We have a large number of supplies, many of which are prone to wander. Bath towels, for instance, are often taken by our guests when they depart."

"Let me know as soon as you have an answer," she said. In the meantime, her partner had a job to do. She knelt beside Rolf and opened the bottle of perfume. The Heartbreaker fragrance filled the air, heavy and sensual. Dabbing a very little of it on a tissue from the bathroom, she held it in front of her K-9's nose.

"Rolf," she said, "*such*."

The perfume on the victim had almost certainly been applied by the killer when he'd dressed her up. He'd have opened it in the room and closed it again before leaving. But that scent would have lingered on him, and just maybe Rolf would be able to find where he'd gone. The smell was almost three days old, but it'd been strong to begin with, and Rolf's nose was pretty damn good.

The Shepherd snorted to clear his nostrils. He cast about for a moment, sniffing the air. Then he put his snout to the carpet and started tracking, tail wagging excitedly. He went straight to the bed, which Erin had expected. Finding no one there, he turned and trotted to the bathroom. He nosed briefly inside, then headed out into the hall. Erin was right there with him, holding his leash but giving him his head.

She thought he'd go to the elevator, then to the lobby and out into the Manhattan streets, where the trail would get lost at whatever point the murderer had gotten into a vehicle. But she was wrong. Rolf went directly to another door. He stopped outside Room 1415, just across the hall and two doors down. He took deep, snuffling breaths at the bottom edge of the door. He scratched at it and whined.

Excitement flooded through Erin. She turned to the hotel manager. "I need to know who rented this room right now."

* * *

Erin called Major Crimes as soon as she had the guest list in hand. She was getting close, she could feel it.

"Precinct 8, Major Crimes," Kira answered.

"This is Erin. I've got a name."

"Is it our guy?"

"I think so," Erin said, tracing the line on the printout next to Room 1415. "Run Bertram Parson for me."

"Just a sec."

Erin heard computer keys clacking. There was a pause.

"Erin? You sure this is the right name?"

Her heart sank. "What's the problem?"

"I've just got one hit."

"Could be our guy, then."

"I doubt it," Kira said. "I'm looking at his obit right now."

"Son of a bitch," Erin muttered. "When did he die?"

"Six weeks ago."

"Maybe our man killed him, took his ID," she suggested.

"Maybe," Kira said doubtfully. "But the obituary says that he, and I quote, 'succumbed after a lengthy battle with bone cancer.'"

Erin wanted to kick the wall. She settled for squeezing her phone as hard as she could. "Maybe the hotel checked his ID," she said.

"There's no legal requirement for a guest to even have ID on him," Kira said. "If he paid cash, he could've been literally anybody. Bin Laden could've gotten a room if he wanted it."

"Bin Laden's dead," Erin reminded her.

"So's Bertram Parson," Kira replied. "Didn't stop him."

"Very funny. You guys having any luck on Rüdel?"

"Nothing yet. The LT and Vic are pounding pavement, trying to find out if any CIs are willing to talk."

"What about Rüdel's guy that we've got in custody?"

"Webb just talked to him at the hospital, through an interpreter. All he learned was a bunch of new German curse words."

"Got anything else?" Erin asked.

"No. Oh! There is one thing."

"What's that?"

"You didn't order an espresso machine, did you?"

Erin blinked. "The hell?"

"It got delivered right after you left," Kira said. "Brand new. Looks pretty sweet. I checked with Facilities, they don't know anything about it."

"Anything on the manifest?"

"Just a one-sentence message, pretty cryptic. It says, 'For drinks you can enjoy on duty.' You know what that means?"

"Yeah," Erin said under her breath. "Cars."

"Sorry, I didn't catch that."

"Never mind. I'll explain later. Do me a favor, could you? Send me Parson's obit and whatever else you can find on the guy."

"You think there's a zombie killing women in New York?"

"No, our killer may have known Parson," Erin said. "I'll be back at the precinct in a while. I still need to look into some stuff here."

According to the guest list, Bertram Parson had checked in a little before nine o'clock. She went to the front desk and flashed her shield to the receptionist. "Ma'am," she said, "I need to know who was on duty between eight and nine in the evening, three nights ago."

The young woman brought up her schedule. "That was Vonnie," she said, cocking her head to the far end of the counter. "She's on duty right now."

Vonnie was a perky blonde in her mid-twenties. When she saw Erin, her face lit up, but she wasn't looking at the detective. "Oh, a puppy!" she exclaimed. "He's adorable!"

Erin raised her eyebrows. Rolf was on duty. "Adorable" wasn't the first word that came to mind. Alert? Focused? Intense? Absolutely. He hadn't been a puppy in years. "Vonnie?" she said, coming face to face with her.

"That's me," Vonnie said cheerfully. "We're a pet-friendly hotel, of course, and your four-legged friend is more than welcome. I love dogs! I have a King Charles Spaniel at home. He's Mommy's little marshmallow, a total cuddlebug!"

"I'm Detective O'Reilly with the NYPD," she said. "Rolf is a police K-9. I just need to ask you a couple of questions about one of your guests."

"Of course," Vonnie said. "Can I pet him?"

Erin couldn't help smiling a little. Compared to some of the payoffs informants wanted, this was pretty small change. "Okay," she said. "But be polite. He's a professional working animal."

"Oh, that is so precious!" Vonnie said. She made a kissy face at Rolf over the countertop. "Who's a good little working dog? I'll bet you're so good at your job, yes you are!"

Rolf looked up at Erin. She knew he was watching for instructions, but she could've sworn he rolled his eyes just a little.

"Vonnie," she said, "do you remember a Bertram Parson? He checked in while you were working, three nights back. About nine in the evening."

The receptionist drummed her fingers on the counter and looked off into space. "I don't think so," she said, her eyes going back to Rolf.

"He probably paid cash," Erin guessed.

"Oh, yeah!" Vonnie said. "I do remember that. Most folks use plastic. But he had exact change. It was kind of weird. He'd even worked out the occupancy tax ahead of time, down to the penny."

That sounded like the behavior of a tidy psycho. "What did he look like?" Erin asked. Her hands were gripping the edge of the counter.

Vonnie shrugged. "He was just a guy."

This wasn't the first time Erin had needed to jog a witness's memory. She started fishing for info. "Was he white? Black? Asian?"

"He was a white guy."

"How tall?"

"I don't know."

"Taller than me?"

Vonnie laughed. She and Erin were about the same height. "What guys aren't taller than us? I guess maybe five-ten or so."

"Was he a big guy? Broad in the shoulders?"

"No, he was kinda thin."

"Good-looking?"

Vonnie grinned at her. "Yeah. He looked nice. Pleasant. He had a good smile. Good hair, you could tell he took care of himself. And kind eyes."

Erin pictured a good-looking man injecting poison into a girl, watching her die. She wondered if his eyes stayed kind while the poison took effect. "What color hair?" she asked.

"Dark. Black or maybe really dark brown. Dark eyes, too."

"How old?"

Vonnie thought about it. "Hard to tell. More than twenty, less than forty?"

"What was he wearing?"

"Sport coat and slacks."

"Color?"

"Khaki pants, dark blue coat," Vonnie said. She remembered more than she'd thought, which wasn't uncommon.

"Necktie?"

"No. Open collar. Button-down shirt under the coat, light blue I think."

"Did you see his hands?"

"Sure. Why?"

"Were there any marks on them? What were his fingernails like?"

"Clean hands, no wedding ring," Vonnie said and giggled. "He'd shaved recently, too. I could smell his cologne. There was another smell on him, too. Faint. Some kind of perfume, maybe?"

"Would you recognize him if you saw him again?" Erin asked.

"Of course. I was kind of hoping I'd run into him." Vonnie giggled again. "We're not supposed to date guests, of course, but I thought if he was only in town for a couple of days, maybe we could go out, have some fun."

"Yeah," Erin said dryly. Her skin was crawling. "I'll bet you're just his type."

"Can I pet him now?" Vonnie asked. She was making baby faces at Rolf again.

"Sure," Erin said. "I'll need you to fill out a statement in a minute, though. Rolf, *sitz*."

Rolf knew his duty. He obediently sat and accepted a few pats on the head.

* * *

A quarter of an hour later, armed with Vonnie's written statement and the manager's promise that he'd e-mail her the list of former employees, Erin left the DoubleTree. She was feeling pretty good. The killer had been clever, but he'd made mistakes. She was closing in. Vonnie had agreed to sit with a sketch artist as soon as her shift ended. Then the NYPD might be able to put a face on the murderer. Lost in her thoughts, she walked toward the police space where she'd left her Charger.

Rolf suddenly froze. Then, wagging his tail, he angled hard right, into the street. Erin's arm was jerked sideways. Caught off guard, she stumbled and nearly fell.

"*Rolf! Hier!*" she snapped, startled, annoyed, and a little scared. Her K-9 was well enough trained to know better than to go haring off in the middle of Manhattan. Fortunately, she'd stopped him before he could lunge into the path of traffic.

The Shepherd briskly returned to stand at her hip, looking up at her. He knew he was being scolded, but he seemed more confused than ashamed. His ears were perked forward and his tail waved uncertainly.

Erin shook her head and smiled down at him. One of the first things they'd taught her in K-9 training was that when a dog misbehaved, it was at least as much the handler's fault. She'd been distracted and had probably given him a signal without meaning to. "It's okay, boy," she told him, rubbing the base of his ears. It was time to get back to the precinct and catch up with the rest of the squad. She loaded Rolf into the back of the car and went to the driver's door.

"Erin?"

It was her turn to freeze in surprise, one hand on the door handle. She knew she recognized the voice, but couldn't place it out of context. Then, just as she saw him, she remembered.

"Trevor?"

The perfume-store clerk was standing on the curb just a few feet away. He had a Smartphone in his hand and a pleasant smile on his face.

"What are you doing here?" she asked.

"Sightseeing," he said with a sheepish little shrug. "I like to walk around Manhattan. I've lived here my whole life, but there's always more to see. Mostly I watch people. What brings you to the neighborhood?"

"Work."

"I hope I was able to help with your investigation," he said.

That earned him a quick smile. "You were. We're on the scent."

"Literally, or figuratively?"

"Both," she said. "That perfume sample may have busted the case open."

Trevor looked at Rolf, who craned his neck toward him but stayed where Erin had told him to, at her side. "Can he really track perfume?"

"Rolf can track anything," she said. "Human scent and explosives are his specialty. Look, Trevor, I'm on the clock here. I'd love to stick around and chat, but I have to get back to the precinct."

"Of course," he said. "Look, Erin, I want to say something about when we spoke on the phone earlier. I hope I didn't make you uncomfortable. I wouldn't want to do that. I'm not very experienced with women, and I may have given you the wrong idea."

"It takes more than that to make me uncomfortable," she said. "You seem like a nice guy, Trevor, but I really am busy right now."

"Maybe I'll see you again. Another chance meeting?"

"Guess we'll find out," she said absently, getting in the car.

Chapter 15

As she pulled out of her parking space, Erin got a text. Ignoring all rules of safe driving, she glanced down at her phone. The message was from Kira and just said "Get back to the office NOW."

That could only mean one thing: Rüdel. Erin engaged her Bluetooth with one hand, activated her flashers with the other, and started moving as fast as possible through downtown Manhattan. This wasn't really very fast, but it was the best she could do.

"You rolling?" were the first words Kira said over the phone.

"On my way," Erin said. "I'm leaving the hotel. I'll be there in fifteen. What's up?"

"We got Rüdel's file. Vic just pulled it off the wires from Interpol. Pictures, history, the works."

"Great," Erin said. "What's our next move?"

"We've already put out a BOLO. Webb's called in reinforcements. We've got uniforms gearing up to canvas pretty much everywhere on the south side of Manhattan. We're gonna put him on the evening news."

"You think that's a good idea?" Erin asked, swerving around

a stubborn pickup truck that pretended not to see her flashing lights. "He sees himself on TV, he's gonna go to ground."

"We need the extra eyes," Kira said. "We haven't got enough bodies to search everywhere, and we've got no idea where he is."

"What does Webb need me to do?"

"Come in now. We'll form up at the precinct."

A motor scooter pizza-delivery guy abruptly swung across Erin's lane, nearly clipping her fender. She swore and hit the brakes, which brought a chorus of irritated honks from other drivers.

"Get off the phone, Erin," Kira advised. "Studies show that using the phone while driving, even hands-free, is comparable to moderate alcoholic impairment. It slows reactions by up to a second."

"Thanks for sharing," Erin snapped. "See you there." She was annoyed not least because Kira was probably right. Driving in Manhattan was dangerous enough already.

*   *   *

Major Crimes was full of police. Uniformed officers, plainclothes detectives, auxiliaries, some doing important jobs, some just milling around. In the middle of it, Erin found Webb talking to Captain Holliday.

"O'Reilly," Webb said. "Glad you're here."

"Sorry to pull you in like this," Holliday said. "I know you're working another important case."

"It's okay, sir," Erin said. She hadn't gotten much chance to know the Captain. He had a reputation as a tough, fair officer, but his management style tended to be pretty hands-off. That he was directing the manhunt in person told her how seriously the NYPD was taking the search. She looked at Webb. "Orders?"

"Take a look at Rüdel's file," he said. "See if anything jumps out at you. From what we've got, I feel like we could find him if he was hiding in Munich, but Manhattan? Damned if I know."

The whiteboard had been updated, but Erin didn't want the bullet-point version. She located Vic and Kira at Vic's desk. They had a bunch of computer printouts spread out in front of them.

"So," Erin said, coming up on Vic's shoulder. "Who is this guy?"

He handed her a scan of a mugshot and the front page of an Interpol file. Erin took it and thanked God Interpol used English as one of its main bureaucratic languages. Her K-9 commands wouldn't help her navigate German bureaucracy. For the first time, she saw Hans Rüdel's face.

She'd been expecting the sort of guy who played SS officers in old World War II movies: blond, blue-eyed, and arrogant. Rüdel's eyes were blue all right, but his hair was brown, buzzed down almost to the scalp. Most perps tried to look badass in their mugshots. Rüdel just looked bored. His eyes were unfocused and hooded, a little sleepy.

Erin scanned his file. Hans Rüdel had packed a lot into his thirty-two years. He was former military, a combat engineer with the *Deutsches Heer*, the German Army. That was good, because it meant they had fingerprints, blood type, and personal history up to the time he'd left the *Heer* ten years earlier. But it was also bad. It meant he had professional military training. "Combat Engineer," combined with the incident at the Barley Corner, indicated Rüdel knew his way around explosives. After getting out of the military, he'd joined an ultranationalist skinhead group, picking up a nice collection of white-supremacist tattoos in the process. He'd done thirteen months in Landsberg Prison for conspiracy to blow up a government building in Munich. While incarcerated, he'd studied electrical engineering.

"The German prison system is designed for rehabilitation," Kira said, looking at the sheet in Erin's hands. "They try to recreate the conditions of outside life for inmates, while protecting society from the prisoners until they're ready to re-enter the regular world."

"Doesn't look like he got very rehabilitated," Vic said dryly. "He was only outside for six months, then he was right back in again."

"Don't judge the system based on him," Kira said. "Germany has a much lower recidivism rate than we do."

Whatever the merits of Germany's criminal-justice system, Rüdel had gotten busted for assault less than a year after his release. He was in and out of prison until '09, after which he'd cleaned up his act, or more likely just avoided getting caught. He was suspected of racketeering, assault, murder, terrorism, hate crimes, and so on down the list, but nothing proven.

"Christ," Erin muttered, flipping through page after page of allegations. "This guy's a real son of a bitch."

"Yeah," Vic said. "And he's here now. If we collar him, you think the Germans will let us keep him? Maybe he'll like Sing Sing better than Landsberg."

Erin got to the section on Rüdel's known associates. There were a lot of names, but all of them were native Germans. There wasn't a thing in the file that hinted at where he might be, who he was working with, or what he planned to do.

"Where the hell is this guy?" she asked, not expecting an answer.

"I think we can rule out Harlem," Vic said.

"No, Vic, a neo-Nazi with a swastika tattooed on his neck is not going to hang out in Harlem," Kira said, rolling her eyes.

Vic made an angry gesture at the pile of paper in front of him. "This is bullshit," he said. "This asshole doesn't belong here. He's not connected to New York wiseguys. Why's he picking off

Scotsmen in New York harbor? He run out of people to kill on the other side of the ocean?"

"I need a cup of coffee," Erin said. She started for the break room, then paused. "Kira, you said there was a new machine."

"Yeah, the guy who brought it already installed it," Kira said. "Truth is, I think that's why half these guys are hanging around on our floor. We've already had to refill it twice. I'll show you."

* * *

Erin could've found the espresso machine by smell alone. After so many years of standard-issue police coffee, it was like her nose had gone from black and white Kansas into technicolor Oz. The machine was state of the art, all shiny stainless steel. A cluster of Patrol officers was lurking around it, bitching about Major Crimes getting all the new equipment. Erin and Kira shooed them away.

As soon as the other officers were out of the break room, Kira closed the door and flipped the deadbolt. Then she crossed her arms and stared at Erin.

"Okay, give," she said. "Start talking. Where'd this thing come from?"

Erin sighed. "I couldn't say for sure. And if it's who I think it is, we'll never be able to prove it. He'll have covered the paper trail too well."

"Laundering a coffee machine?" Kira snorted. "That's a new one. He a mob boss, or what?"

There was a moment of silence.

"Oh, shit," Kira said. "You're telling me this machine's a gift from *Morton fucking Carlyle?*"

Erin nodded. "A little thank-you for saving his life and his bar. Again."

"Great. Just great. We're getting kickbacks from the Irish Mob now." Kira leaned against the wall and ran a hand through her hair.

"So what do you want me to do? You want to send it back?"

"No, I don't want to send it back. It gave me the best damn cup of coffee I've had in a month! That's not the point!"

"What is the point?" Erin asked. "You don't need to tell me Carlyle's playing me. He danced all over the place when I tried to pin him down about Rüdel. He kept going on about how he couldn't tell me anything. I don't know why he was even talking to me in the first place!" Fuming, she turned to the machine and poured herself a cup of coffee. For a few seconds she just held it and enjoyed the smell, getting a handle on her emotions. Then she tried a sip. Kira was right. It was the best coffee she'd ever had in a police station.

Kira hadn't replied. Erin looked up from her drink. The other woman was watching her thoughtfully.

"I wasn't undercover with the gang task force," Kira said. "It was more a sort of community-outreach thing. I tried to find out why boys got channeled into gang culture, worked on getting them out of the life. Spinning wheels, mostly. It's hard to pry them loose once they're in, and they get in early. Sometimes I'd meet kids who were ten, twelve years old, already in the system.

"One of the biggest issues when dealing with gangs is that no one's willing to talk to the police," she went on. "If word gets out that one of the gang's talking to the cops, next thing you know, Patrol's fishing him out of a dumpster with a hole in his head."

"Yeah, I know," Erin said. "So why'd Carlyle want to talk to me?"

"I've been thinking about that," Kira said. She made a wry face. "I always think about how somebody in an organization may be trying to work the system. It's an Internal Affairs reflex,

I guess. This is the second time you've stopped something major going down in Carlyle's bar. He couldn't pretend it was coincidence."

"But it *was* coincidence!" Erin protested. "They were totally unrelated cases. If I'd known Rüdel was going to hit the Corner, I'd have had ESU there. Hell, I'd at least have been wearing my vest!"

"Not the point," Kira said again. "You think anybody in the O'Malleys would believe that? Think about how it looks to them."

Erin thought about it. "It looks like Carlyle's got police cover."

"And since he doesn't really have it, he hasn't told the other O'Malleys about it," Kira said.

"Right," Erin said. "Evan O'Malley probably thinks Carlyle's been hiding this from him. And that makes him look bad to his boss."

"So Carlyle couldn't pretend there was nothing going on," Kira said. "He had to talk to you, but not alone. That would only cause more suspicion."

"That's why Corky was there," Erin said, snapping her fingers. "Carlyle needed a witness."

"Yeah," Kira said. "But isn't Corcoran one of Carlyle's best friends?"

Erin nodded. "So?"

"So he's already on Carlyle's side. Which means maybe Carlyle did want to tell you something after all."

Erin put down her coffee cup to rub her temples. "Now I'm just confused."

"Carlyle went to the trouble of setting up a meet, in front of one of his friends," Kira said. "A friend who would probably lie for him if he asked him to. All so he could tell you he didn't know anything about the guy who tried to kill him."

"Wait," Erin said. "That's not what he said."

"Well, something like that," Kira said. "It doesn't matter—"

"No," Erin interrupted. "It does matter, because Carlyle doesn't ever say anything he doesn't mean to. He's the most careful man with his words I've ever met. He's like a criminal politician."

"Aren't all politicians criminal?" Kira retorted.

"Ha ha. Be quiet a second. This is important." Erin racked her brain to recall the exact words. "I asked who was writing Rüdel's checks. He said, 'I can't possibly answer that.' I asked, 'Can't, or won't?'"

"What'd he say?"

"He asked if the distinction was important."

Kira smiled. "I'd like to get this guy in an interrogation room sometime, see what I could shake out of him."

"I know the feeling," Erin said. "He didn't answer. I pressed him and asked flat-out whether he knew who'd hired Rüdel. He said no. Then I asked who he thought had done it, and he said he couldn't say."

"Where's that leave you?"

"I think," Erin said slowly, "he wanted to tell me. I think he wanted me to know he wanted to tell me."

"But he didn't tell you."

"Nope." Erin sighed. "So maybe you're right, maybe it doesn't matter."

Kira was shaking her head. "Hold on," she said. "Has he been helping you with the other case?"

"Yeah. But he doesn't know anything concrete. He's more of a... technical adviser, I guess."

"So he'll help you with police work."

"Sometimes, yeah."

"Why not this time?"

"He likes being difficult, playing games with me."

"He could get killed for talking to you at all, Erin. What are we missing here?"

Then Erin got it. She just had to stop thinking like a police detective and start thinking like a mobster. From Carlyle's perspective, it was obvious. "You're right," she said. "The O'Malleys will kill him if he squeals on them. So he can't."

"Okay," Kira said. "But the O'Malleys are the ones getting attacked."

"No! *Carlyle* is getting attacked. I think he's been targeted by someone inside his own organization. Using an outsider, so it's harder to trace back."

"Yeah," Kira said. "He wants it known that he's not betraying the O'Malleys, so he said, in front of a witness, that he couldn't help you. But he said it in a way that you'd know what he wanted to say."

"He's got a pretty high opinion of my logic, if he figured all this ahead of time," Erin muttered. "But if we're right, then we know where Rüdel is. Sort of. One of Carlyle's internal rivals in the O'Malleys is hiding him."

"It's thin," Kira said. "I don't think we can get warrants on the basis of what a criminal isn't telling us."

"But we can focus our search," Erin said. "The O'Malleys operate in southern Manhattan and northern Queens. Rüdel's there somewhere. I'd bet on it."

"That's still a lot of territory," Kira said doubtfully.

"It's a start," Erin said. "So, is my interrogation over?"

Kira laughed and unbolted the door. She opened it and found herself face to face with Sergeant Brown.

"You two ladies finished screwing each other?" he asked. "You could at least leave the door open next time so the rest of us can watch. You willing to let a Vice cop try a cup of decent coffee?"

Kira smiled sweetly, gave him the finger, and stepped

around the Vice sergeant. "See you around, Brown," she said. "Some of us have work to do."

Chapter 16

"I know it's thin, sir," Erin finished. "But—"

"Thin?" Webb echoed. "O'Reilly, skim milk is thin. Piano wire is thin. Hell, back in high school, *I* was thin. This? This is two-dimensional."

Erin started to protest, but Webb wasn't finished yet.

"It's not a hunch," he went on. "It's a hunch, based on another hunch you think Carlyle has, which you think he told you, by not really telling you. Have I got that right?"

Sometimes there was nothing to do but face the music. Erin stood at parade rest, hands clasped behind her back, looking straight ahead. "Yes, sir."

The Lieutenant sighed. "We're putting his face out on the evening news. Full-court press. Captain's orders. What do you think you can get done by then?"

She glanced at the clock. "That's less than two hours from now."

"What about it? You still think Rüdel will go to ground when he sees his picture?"

"Yeah, I do."

"You've got until then to see if you can dig up anything better."

"You're giving me two hours to find one guy in Manhattan?"

"Or Queens," Webb added.

"Thanks," she said, managing to keep most of the sarcasm out of her voice. "I better get on it."

Kira and Rolf were waiting for her at her desk. "What's the word?" Kira asked.

"If we don't find him by six thirty, he'll hide somewhere so dark and deep, we'll need dynamite and a team of coal miners to dig him out," Erin said. "That's assuming he's even still in New York."

"Maybe he's not," Kira said. "He's an out of town hit man, right? He always meant to go home after taking Carlyle out."

"Yeah."

"So how's he getting out?" Kira smiled. "You don't have to follow a guy if you know where he's going."

"He's not going by air," Erin said. "Rüdel wouldn't want to mess with the TSA after shooting someone. He's on Homeland's watchlist because of the terrorist thing in Munich. I'm guessing he'll go out the same way he got in."

"Boat?"

"Boat."

"Okay." Kira shrugged. "I dunno if you noticed, but unfortunately, New York's made of islands."

"I know," Erin said absently, sliding into her chair and calling up the case information on her computer. She was looking for Captain MacIntosh's statement. "Apparently, Rüdel used a cigarette boat for his hijack. Fast, fairly short-range."

"He didn't cross the Atlantic in one of those," Kira said.

"No," Erin agreed. "He's probably planning to hop along the coast to another port and get on a cargo ship."

"Why not just use a ship here? New York's got hundreds."

Erin nodded. "Okay, maybe he comes in as a passenger, picks up the little boat here, and uses it to intercept the *Loch Druich*. Then he comes back and gets on another ship heading back to Europe, or wherever he wants to end up."

"That doesn't help," Kira said. "He could be on any ship in the harbor."

"No," Erin said. She was playing her hunch based on Carlyle, so she needed to think like one of the O'Malleys. "Rüdel wouldn't chance being on just any ship. He's on an O'Malley ship."

"They've got ships?"

"I expect they've got a lot of things," Erin said. "But they're smugglers, so yeah, they've got ships. What we need to do is to figure out which of the O'Malleys has access to shipping, and also wants to take out Carlyle."

Kira shook her head. "We've got a big file on the O'Malleys. They've been operating for decades, and there's a bunch of them. It'll take days to sort through it all."

"We've got," Erin looked at the clock again, "an hour to do the research, tops, and still have time to run down a lead or two."

"We can't delay it going out to the networks?"

"I don't think so," Erin said. To be honest, putting Rüdel's name and picture out was probably a good idea. They only needed to get lucky once to nail him, and having eight million pairs of eyes on their side would help. But she couldn't shake the feeling that Rüdel was clever enough to get out of sight and stay there, that this was their chance. "Wouldn't matter anyway. He's gonna be gone soon, unless he's planning to make another play for Carlyle."

"You think he'd try that again?"

"No. Carlyle's on guard now. He's protected. I saw all sorts of thugs at Corky's place."

"Corky?"

"Corcoran," Erin corrected herself.

"Oh, right. Carlyle's buddy." Kira moved to her own desk. "I'll see what I can skim from the O'Malley file."

* * *

Detectives, Erin had found, spent an awful lot of time staring at computer screens. She wasn't the quickest at gathering information off files and reports. Being on a clock didn't help either. She was trying to learn the ins and outs of a major criminal organization in the space of a few minutes. This would normally be the outcome of a months-long investigation.

As it turned out, the O'Malley file was long on size but short on substance. The NYPD hadn't made any serious effort to shut them down. There was a laundry list of names, all of them linked to various aspects of the family, but the overall picture was blurry.

"We gotta get at someone on the inside," she muttered. There wasn't any substitute for having an officer working the human angle. Informants and undercover work were best.

"Got anything?" Kira called over. They'd used up most of their self-imposed time limit.

"Jack," Erin said, "and maybe his buddy, shit."

"Looks like the Organized Crime unit thinks Corcoran's behind most of the smuggling," Kira said. "Maybe he moved Rüdel."

"I don't think so," Erin said. "Cork—Corcoran's the only guy I think Carlyle really trusts with his life. Carlyle's staying with him right now, for God's sake. If Corcoran's got it in for him, Carlyle would probably already be dead."

"Okay," Kira said. "Then he wouldn't be using any of Corcoran's guys either. Corcoran's plugged in with the Teamsters and the ILA."

"But the Longshoremen's Association moves everything that comes into this city, practically," Erin said. Her dad was a big supporter of labor unions and had made sure his children knew how important they were to New York.

"Exactly," Kira said. "So we're looking for a small, non-union operation affiliated with the O'Malleys."

"How many options does that give us?"

"Too many," Kira said. "How lucky do you feel?"

"Hey, Vic!" Erin called.

"What?" Vic was at his desk, staring at his computer screen as if he could kill the Internet with his eyes.

"You want to knock on some doors, maybe find this asshole?"

He stood up. "Hell, yes."

"Not just yet," Kira said. "We still need to find out which doors to knock on."

Vic's face fell. He slumped back into his chair. "So, what're you gonna do? Play blindfold darts with a map?"

Kira had called up the Port Authority's records. "Not quite," she said. "We're looking for a dock with a ship bound for Europe. Rüdel's going to be headed for home. Cross-reference for non-union longshoremen..." She kept typing. "God, I wish I hadn't given up smoking."

Erin and Vic waited.

"O'Malley connections," Kira went on, flipping through the gang's file. "O'Malleys not connected to Corcoran..."

"You really think this is gonna work?" Vic asked Erin.

She shrugged. "Best chance we've got."

"There," Kira said, pointing to her map. "Off Columbia Street, Brooklyn. This cargo dock." She hesitated. "Or, this other one. Or maybe over in Jamaica Bay. Or..."

"Oh, for Christ's sake," Vic said.

"I can't help it," Kira said. "It's not like there's a neon sign pointing to the right answer. None of this is collated. I'm doing it in my head, dammit!"

"So, we each take one of these?" Vic suggested.

"No," Erin said. "Rüdel's dangerous. And last we knew he's got at least one friend with him. If were sure where he was, we'd want ESU. We need to pick one and check it out together. We can probably get some uniforms to go for the other sites, too, but we can't grab too many resources off the street. Like Webb said, it's a hunch based on a hunch."

"Shouldn't we get some more backup?" Kira asked.

"What for?" Vic replied. "All we know, this asshole's ten miles from any of these places. Face it, Erin, you're shooting in the dark."

"Yeah," she admitted. "But what else can we do? What's your best guess, Kira? Off this list?"

"Why me?"

"You're our best data analyst."

"Okay, Columbia Street it is," Kira said. "Here, on the East River."

*　　*　　*

They took two cars, Erin and Rolf in her Charger, Kira and Vic in Kira's Taurus. The arrangement left Erin to wrestle with her thoughts during the drive. She was thinking about Rüdel, but she was also thinking about the hotel killer. And most of all, strangely, she was thinking about Carlyle. She couldn't prove it, couldn't even explain it in a way that made sense, but she knew he was trying to help her. She found herself wanting to trust him more than the situation warranted.

Either she was right or she wasn't. Even if she was right, maybe he wasn't. Erin was uncomfortably aware just how big the Five Boroughs were. She also knew how many people lived in New York. It was rush hour and the bridges were packed. Fortunately, as police on official business, they could use the bus and bike lanes. Since their cars were unmarked, not all their fellow New Yorkers recognized them as cops. They collected some rude gestures and irritable honks along the way.

Erin liked Long Island. She'd been born there and had spent almost her entire police career in Queens. The blue-collar feel of the place was a lot more comfortable to her than the skyscraper canyons of Manhattan. This was her hometown, her people.

The two cars drew up at the dockyard. A chain-link fence surrounded the yard, topped with a coil of razorwire. On the other side they could see big, bright-colored cargo containers that reminded Erin of the blocks she and her brothers had played with as kids. The parking lot inside was almost empty. Two cars were parked there, a black Lexus and a silver Suburban SUV.

Vic and Kira got out of Kira's car and walked back to meet Erin. Kira was working the Velcro fasteners on her vest. Vic was already wearing his. Erin took a moment to put Rolf's body armor on him, then geared herself up. She was carrying a loaner Glock from the precinct's armory. Her own sidearm was still being held as evidence in the Barley Corner shootout, but that didn't bother her. One Glock was pretty much the same as another.

"We can't go in there without a warrant," Kira said.

"Pop the trunk, would you?" Vic said, ignoring her words. Kira flicked the button on her key fob. Vic took out the M4 carbine he'd stowed there, slapped a magazine into the rifle, and chambered a round.

"You could at least pretend to listen to me," Kira said. "Because I'm right. That's private property. We need PC to go in, and we don't have it."

"I'm just getting ready," Vic said. "In case."

"Seems kinda quiet, doesn't it?" Erin observed.

The others looked around. Kira nodded. "Yeah, where is everyone?"

Cars were passing on Columbia, but the dockyard itself looked deserted. The work day was about over, true, but there still should've been a few workers around.

"Whose cars are those, you think?" Vic asked.

"Got me," Kira said.

"Can you make out the plates from here?" he went on.

"Vic, it's not like we're going to find Rüdel listed in the DMV database," Kira said. "He didn't bring a car from Germany."

"No, he didn't," Erin said, getting it. "But he's not buying cars or renting them, either."

"Meaning?" Kira asked.

Erin didn't explain right away. "Alpha Golf Bravo six eight niner three, I make it," she said, squinting to see the SUV's rear plate.

"I got the same," Vic said. "Tango Mike Echo eight oh thirty-three on the sedan."

"I'll run them," Kira said, climbing back into her car. "But I still don't see—"

"If they're being used by Rüdel, they're probably stolen," Erin explained. "And that's our probable cause."

"Oh," Kira said. "Geez. I feel like an idiot."

Inside three minutes, she'd run both plates. "I got nothing on the Lexus," she said. "But the Suburban was reported stolen yesterday."

"Beautiful," Vic said quietly. "Let's rock." The difference in him was palpable. The surly, grumpy desk jockey had come alive. He was doing what he'd been put on Earth to do.

"Hold on," Kira said. "We can get ESU now, right?"

Erin hesitated. Kira might be right. But they still weren't sure. Right now, all they had was a stolen car in a Mob-affiliated parking lot. That was good enough to go in, but not to get a whole squad of door-kickers. Besides, that would take time, and in that time Rüdel might be gone... assuming he was even there.

"Let's do this," she said.

"Erin, seriously," Kira said. "I've got a bad feeling about this."

"Stay with the cars," Vic said to her. "Call it in, get some uniforms, direct them in after us. Erin and I will go in."

"And Rolf," Erin added.

"And Rolf," Vic agreed. Holding his rifle against his shoulder, barrel angled slightly down, head scanning for threats, he moved to the gate. Erin drew her Glock, press-checked the pistol to make sure a round was chambered, and followed.

"Careful, guys," Kira called after them.

"Careful?" Vic repeated. "If I wanted to be careful, I'd have done what Mom wanted and become a florist."

"A florist?" Erin echoed.

"She thought it'd be a good way for me to meet girls," he said defensively.

"She's probably right," Erin admitted.

They looked at each other. Then, some combination of the strange conversation topic and the tension of the moment hit them and they both started laughing. Kira was staring at them like they were crazy, and Erin thought maybe they were, a little. Then they got themselves under control.

"Hey!" Vic shouted. "You in there! NYPD! We're coming in. Hands where we can see them!"

Chapter 17

There was no response from the dockyard. Vic covered the grounds with his rifle while Erin checked the gate.

"It's not locked," she said.

"Makes sense," he grunted. "In case they need to get out fast."

She put her shoulder to the chain-link barrier and shoved it back on its rollers. She opened it halfway, leaving it that way to prevent a vehicle's exit. Kira, behind the wheel of her car, moved the Taurus to block the road.

"I've got your back," Vic said. "Go."

Erin sprinted across the parking lot, Rolf running easily at her side. She got to the parked cars and gave them a quick once-over. No one was inside.

"Clear!" she called to Vic, then crouched behind the Suburban's engine block, keeping it between her and the dock.

Once she was set up, Vic came in. It was a game of armed leapfrog. He took position behind the Lexus. "Where the hell are they?" he wondered.

Erin considered the problem. The dock itself was empty. A ship was scheduled to leave the following day, but it wasn't anchored there now. Someone could easily be hiding among the stacked containers, or even inside one, but there were dozens of the huge metal crates. They'd need twenty cops to canvas the area.

Twenty cops, or one K-9.

"Rolf!" Erin said. The Shepherd was watching her intently, waiting for orders. She pointed to the Suburban's door handle. "*Such!*"

Rolf went up on his hind paws and sniffed the handle with deep, snuffling breaths. Then he dropped back to the pavement, put his nose to the ground, and was off toward the steel jungle of cargo crates.

Vic followed about ten yards behind and a little to one side, keeping his M4 at his shoulder. They crossed the remainder of the parking lot and started in among the piled containers.

It was a tactical nightmare. Visibility was twenty yards or less in any direction. An enemy could be in front, to either side, or even above. She tried to look everywhere at once, telling herself not to give in to paranoia.

Kira was right. They should've waited for backup. They needed more officers on site. Even two or three more pairs of eyes would make things a lot safer. She pulled on Rolf's leash. "*Hier!*" she ordered. It was time to call him back before someone got hurt.

Rolf stopped, but he was quivering with excitement. He barked twice, sharply.

"We're close," Erin said to Vic. "I think maybe—"

Metal crashed just around the corner. A cargo container's door had been flung open, rebounding off the one next to it. She reflexively craned her neck to look.

"Get back!" Vic snapped. At the same moment there was a sound like a strip of cloth being torn. A line of jagged holes marched diagonally up the container wall where she'd been about to put her head.

Submachine-gun, Erin thought distractedly. She backed away from the corner, Glock leveled. Rolf came with her, obeying her last instruction.

"Kira! Call in a 10-13!" Vic shouted. "Erin, watch that corner!" Then he pointed to himself and gestured around the far end of the container.

She nodded her understanding. He was outflanking the bad guy. She turned her attention back to the corner in time to see more bullet holes punch through the the steel.

The shooter wasn't trying to hit her. Erin remembered that Rüdel was former military. He was using infantry tactics, laying down suppressing fire. She was no soldier, but she knew what that meant. Rüdel was trying to pin them in place while he moved. The only question was whether he was trying to attack or retreat.

Vic paused an instant, then went around the opposite corner and out of Erin's line of sight. "Drop it!" he shouted. Less than a second later, she heard three flat, hard cracks from a rifle. A man cried out.

"Rolf! *Fass!*" Erin called, slipping the K-9 loose from his leash. He leaped forward. Erin followed him.

A guy lay on the pavement, clutching his thigh. An MP5K submachine-gun had fallen next to him, surrounded by spent brass. Vic stood at the other end of the passage between two containers, sighting down the barrel of his rifle. Even as Erin took in the scene, Rolf launched himself at the downed man and latched onto his right arm, exactly the way he'd been trained. The unlucky perp suddenly discovered that a bullet in the leg was nothing compared to almost a hundred pounds of German Shepherd coming at him teeth-first. He started screaming.

Vic raised the muzzle of his gun to take her and Rolf out of his field of fire. "Clear," he said. "Is that him?"

Erin kicked the gun away from the wounded man and stood over him, covering with her pistol. She saw a square-jawed face with a couple days' rough stubble on the chin. The guy was big, muscular, blond. She'd never seen his face before.

"No," she said to Vic.

"Ah, shit," he said. He began to turn away.

Two pistol shots echoed through the dockyard. Vic staggered back against a container wall, only the sheet of steel keeping him on his feet. He brought up his M4 and fired, almost in reflex, at something Erin couldn't see.

"Vic!" she screamed. Ignoring the wounded perp at her feet, she ran toward her fellow detective.

Two more shots sounded. She didn't see where one of them went, but the other left a hole in the metal less than an inch from Vic's ear. He cursed, braced himself against the side of the cargo crate, and fired again.

Erin did something she'd seen in plenty of action movies, but had never thought she'd do for real. She went into a forward roll, staying low to keep out of Vic's line of fire, and came up on one knee, pistol held in both hands, aiming down the barrel. She saw a short space of open ground and a concrete walkway beside the pier. On the concrete, right at the water's edge, stood Hans Rüdel. The range was about fifteen yards. The German had a gun in one hand. The other was pressed to his side. There was blood on his fingers.

She started to yell at him to drop the gun, but at that moment he and Vic both fired. Vic's bullet hit Rüdel in the upper part of his chest, just below the shoulder. The impact spun him around. Rüdel stumbled backward and fell, almost in slow motion, off the dock and into the East River.

Vic tried to hold himself upright, but one of his feet slipped. He started going down. Erin, turning, saw him and managed to get an arm around him. She'd forgotten how heavy he was. She slowed his fall, but he dragged her down with him. They ended up sitting next to each other on the ground.

Erin snatched out her phone to call Dispatch. "O'Reilly, shield four-nine-four-oh," she gasped out. "I have a 10-13. Officer down!"

"Stop it, Erin," Vic muttered. "Quit being so goddamn dramatic. I'm fine."

"O'Reilly," Dispatch said. "Officers are already inbound."

"There's no officer down," Vic protested. "I'm good."

"You've been shot, dumbass!" Erin snapped.

"Vest stopped the round," he said. "Just got my breath knocked out. Gimme a minute."

She could hear sirens. That was probably the backup Kira had called in. She checked Vic for blood and didn't find any. He did have two slugs embedded in his vest, center mass. Tight grouping, two inches apart, just below the heart. Rüdel was one hell of a shot.

"Lucky bastard," she said, trying to cover up the rush of relief. "He could've been aiming for the head."

"See? Told you, I'm fine."

"Keep still," she said. "You might have a couple cracked ribs."

"Whatever you say, Mom," he said and smiled. It was strange. She hadn't seen Vic look that happy in weeks.

After that, once the Patrol units arrived, it was all cleanup.

* * *

Later, after Rüdel's wounded henchman was hauled off to the hospital under police guard, after the detectives' statements, after ten carloads of Patrol officers and a van of CSU techs swarmed all over the docks, looking for Rüdel's body, Erin found Kira sitting on the edge of the pier. The other woman's legs were dangling over the water. Her hands were clasped between her knees and she was staring at her own fingers.

Erin took a seat beside her. "You okay?"

"I don't know," Kira said.

They were quiet for a few moments.

"Vic's fine," Erin said at last. "He's hardly hurt."

"That's good."

"And he tagged Rüdel," Erin went on.

Kira nodded. "Not that it matters," she said.

"What the hell are you talking about? Of course it matters! It's why we were there!"

"To kill another mope?"

"What? No!"

"But that's what happened."

"That was Rüdel's choice," Erin said. "He could've given up. They shoot at us, we have to shoot back."

"This isn't why I became a cop," Kira said.

"Kira, nobody puts on their shield in the morning hoping they get to shoot somebody," Erin said. "But it's always a risk. Rüdel was a nasty piece of work. He and his goons killed four people that we know about. They nearly got me twice, plus Vic, not even counting Carlyle and those other folks at the Corner."

"That's what I mean," Kira said. She looked up. Her eyes were haunted. "I'm scared, Erin. All the time. I should've gone in with you and Vic, but I just couldn't."

"Someone needed to cover the exit," Erin said.

"I don't think I'm cut out for this," Kira said. "Look at Vic. He's been through the same shit we have, worse even, but he keeps kicking down doors because he *wants* to. I guess I'm just a desk jockey when the chips are down. Even on the task force, I wasn't making arrests. Shit, Erin, this isn't me!"

"Look, Kira," Erin said. "Most officers don't ever fire their guns in the line. We've been in how many shootouts this summer? This is crazy. Things have to calm down soon."

"What if they don't?" There were tears in Kira's eyes. "What am I gonna do? What are you gonna do? You have to be able to count on me. What if I can't be there for you? Maybe I should put in for a transfer."

"We couldn't have cracked this without you," Erin said. She put a hand on Kira's shoulder. "We need you here. Don't do anything sudden. Take a couple days, let this settle. Okay?"

"If you say so," Kira said. "I don't know how you do it."

"Neither do I," Erin admitted. "I just see what needs doing, and I do it."

"You have to turn in your loaner gun?"

"No," Erin said. "I never fired a shot. Bad angles, bad timing."

"Think they'll find Rüdel's body soon?"

"They're bringing in divers," Erin said. "The water's pretty murky, but bodies usually float. I expect he'll wash up in a day or two, if they don't find him sooner."

"You don't think..." Kira began.

"That he made it?" Erin thought about it. "Not likely. Vic hit him at least twice with rifle rounds, close range. He'd have had a hell of a time swimming away."

"Yeah," Kira said. "You're right. I'm worrying too much. I'm a bundle of goddamn nerves. Think the medics would give me a trank shot if I asked?"

"You looking to get busted by the narc squad?"

"Guess not." Kira stood up. "I'd better get back to the precinct. This dockyard is run by the O'Malleys, but I don't know who specifically. Maybe I can figure out who Rüdel's employer was. Then you and Vic can go arrest somebody else, or maybe shoot him."

"Ha ha," Erin said. "Vic's not shooting anybody right now. He's going on administrative leave. Again. I expect the Lieutenant will send me home, too. Think you can handle Webb on your own for a day or so?"

"I got a choice?" Kira made a face. "Hey, thanks, Erin. And I'm sorry."

"Save it," Erin said. Then, to her surprise, Kira stepped in close and gave her a quick, tight hug. Before she could say anything else, the other woman turned and hurried away.

*   *   *

"There goes my ride," Vic said, watching Kira's Taurus roll out.

"No problem," Erin said. "I'll give you a lift. I won't even make you ride in the dog compartment."

"Whatever. We done here?"

Erin caught Webb's eye. "Hey, Lieutenant! What else can we do?"

"Nothing right now," Webb said. He'd been talking to the detective in charge of the Crime Scene Unit. The CSU guys were unpacking floodlights. The sun was going down, and they were getting ready for the long haul. "Go on home, get some sleep. We'll need you back in the office in the morning to go over your statements again."

"The hell for?" Vic said. "We're not gonna change a word. What happened, happened."

"How many men have the two of you shot over the past two months?" Webb retorted. "You had to stop and count, right? That's a bad sign. We're going to play this one clean and careful. No screwups. The press will be all over it anyway."

"I hate reporters," Vic muttered.

Webb approached and laid a hand on Vic's upper arm. "Neshenko, you did a hell of a job here. This shooting was clean as they come."

"It was Kira and Erin figured it out," Vic said.

"And you put the bastard down," Erin said. "It was a team effort."

"Right," Webb said. "And that's how it'll look in my report. But for now, get away from this crime scene. You see the news vans parked down the street? Drive right past them, don't say a damn word. I'll talk to the Captain and he'll talk to the press. You've done plenty for one day."

"Day's not over yet," Vic said. But he went with Erin and Rolf.

Chapter 18

"So, where do you live, anyway?" Erin asked as they started rolling. "I hope you're not expecting a lift to Newark or something."

"Lower East Side, same as you," Vic said. "Shitty little apartment, costs more than a McMansion's mortgage anywhere else."

"How's your chest?"

He snorted. "Medic says I might've cracked a rib. If I didn't, I don't need to do anything. If I did, I can't do anything. So it doesn't matter."

"Of course it matters, Vic. You got *shot. Twice.*"

"I've been shot before."

"If someone chopped off your leg, and then a couple years later they came back and cut off the other, would you say, 'It's no big deal, I've lost a leg before?'"

He snorted again. "I've heard prosthetics are getting better."

"So, once you get home, what are you planning on doing?" she asked.

"I figured I'd turn on the TV and watch reruns of '24' while drinking straight from the bottle."

"What's in the bottle?"

"Vodka."

"You sure that's a good idea?" Erin tried to keep the concern out of her voice, but a little of it slipped out.

"I just killed a guy. What the hell am I gonna drink, goddamn Coca-Cola?"

"No, but straight vodka? Vic, I've gotta teach you to appreciate good Scotch."

"Hey, you're Irish, I'm Russian. We have to keep in touch with the mother country."

"Right," Erin said. She was watching the road, but her thoughts were all on her partner. Vic had come alive for the gunfight, but now he was in worse shape than before. She wasn't a psych guy, but he had something dark in his mind. She didn't have the first idea how to help him. But then, she wasn't exactly the most stable, well-adjusted officer in the NYPD herself. So she let the silence carry them as far as the Brooklyn Bridge.

"I could use a drink," she heard herself say as they started across the river. "You want to go grab one?"

"Where? I don't want to hit a goddamn cop bar right now," Vic said. "It's gonna be all over the force by now, happy assholes slapping me on the back for what a good job I did, wanting to buy me drinks."

"A drink you don't have to pay for is the best kind," Erin said, thinking of Carlyle and the Corner.

"Yeah," Vic said. "Except whenever some jerk buys you one, you just know he's looking for a way to fuck you."

Erin couldn't help laughing. "You mean that literally?"

"Whatever way you want it," he said. "Everyone in this city, Erin. Christ, everyone on Earth, they're all out to screw you over."

"That's not true."

"Oh yeah? Look what happened with the last girl I thought was into me."

So that was it. Vic's previous girlfriend had been manipulated into setting him up to be killed. She hadn't had much of a choice, but Vic had taken it about as badly as most guys would.

"Vic, we deal with bad guys all the time," she said. "It screws up our worldview. There's plenty of good people out there. We just don't come in contact with them so much."

"Yeah? Name one," Vic said.

"Shelley," Erin said without thinking.

"Who's Shelley?"

"My sister-in-law, Michelle. Married to my brother the doctor. Stay-at-home mom, two kids. The sweetest, friendliest person in the world. Believes the best of everybody."

"What's she think of the Job?"

"You think I want her anywhere near the Job?" Erin retorted. "People like her are why we put on the shield. So they don't have to see all the heinous shit we put up with."

"All I've got is a kid brother," Vic said. "Total screwup. He's in LA, far as I know. Keeps getting taken in for little shit, drug stuff mostly."

"Having a cop for a big brother didn't straighten him out?"

"Probably made it worse." Vic stared out the windshield at the Manhattan skyline. This lights had come on in the dusk, skyscrapers glowing in the gathering night. "You know, I did three years with ESU before transferring to Major Crimes. Never shot anybody while I was there."

"That's not surprising," Erin said. "Most officers don't."

"You tagged that guy outside the art museum during that art heist, back when you were still doing Patrol."

"I only winged him. He lived."

"Now, in Major Crimes, this shit happens all the time," Vic said. "Wild goddamn West."

"If you'd known it'd be like this coming in, what would you have done?"

"Same thing. I just would've liked to know what to expect."

"So, about that drink..." Erin said.

"If you want to try vodka, good Russian imported stuff, you could come by I guess."

"Sounds good," Erin said. "I'll just drop Rolf off at my place."

He hesitated. "Going back to my place, I don't mean..."

She blinked. "Of course not." She never thought of Vic as anything but a partner and a friend.

"Okay then." He clearly wasn't comfortable with that line of conversation. Erin wasn't either, so she was glad to let it drop.

She parked in the police space near her apartment, knowing she wasn't going to be there long. "You can wait here, or you can come up. It'll just be a minute."

"I'll come up," he said. "Better make sure no psycho junkies are waiting to mug you."

"To mug the armed NYPD detective and her K-9?" Erin asked, raising her eyebrows.

"Hey, you never know."

* * *

The apartment building was still and quiet. Erin, Rolf, and Vic walked up to the third floor, shoes clicking on the steps. When they came in sight of Erin's door, they paused. A gift bag stood in front of it. It was dark red with red tissue paper sticking out the top.

"Hold on," Vic said as Erin started forward.

"Give me a second," she said. "Rolf, *such!*"

Rolf put his snout to the ground and snuffled his way up the hallway. He gave the bag a quick sniff. He paused a moment, nostrils quivering.

"Get away from that," Vic growled. He had his hand on his phone, ready to call in the bomb squad. Police officers weren't fond of surprise gifts on their doorsteps.

But Rolf didn't alert to the presence of explosives. He lowered his nose back to the floor, tail wagging, and started back the way they'd come.

"Rolf. *Bleib!*" Erin ordered. The K-9 stopped at once. "It's clean," she said to Vic.

"Okay," he said doubtfully. "I'd still be careful."

Erin cautiously peered into the bag. She saw something round sticking straight up. For a second she wondered about a booby-trap, maybe a sawed-off gun barrel, but then recognized it.

"It's a bottle," she said. She gently took hold of one end of the tissue paper and pulled it free, revealing the contents of the bag.

Vic came closer, peering past her. "What's in it?"

Erin stooped and picked it up. "Irish whiskey," she said, laughing suddenly. "Jameson."

"It been opened?"

She tried to wiggle the cork. "Doesn't feel like it."

"Looks like you've got an admirer," Vic said. "One who knows you pretty well."

"Yeah," Erin said. Still holding the bottle in one hand, she took out her keys and unlocked her door. "C'mon in."

Vic picked up the gift bag and followed her inside.

"I just need to feed Rolf, then we can head out," she said, unfastening the dog's leash and taking off his vest. Rolf, knowing what came next, went into the kitchen and stood expectantly in front of the kibble cupboard.

Erin scooped his dinner into his bowl and set it on the floor. Rolf started chowing down. It'd been a long day and he was hungry.

"You want me to try whiskey, maybe we can crack this one open," Vic said, pointing to the bottle of Jameson. "Looks nice. Expensive. Who do you suppose gave it to you, anyway?"

"Carlyle, probably," Erin said absentmindedly.

"What? Jesus!" Vic stepped back from the bottle as if he'd found a human eyeball floating inside. "You getting booze from gangsters?"

"It's not like that," she said. "His world runs on favors. I saved his life when Rüdel and his goons shot up the Barley Corner. He doesn't want to owe a cop, so he's trying to pay me back."

Vic scanned the gift bag. "The tag isn't signed," he said. "There's no note or anything."

"Of course not. He knows I can't accept anything from him."

"But you know it's from him."

"But I can't prove it." She sighed. "That's the point."

"If you say so. Does he really think a bottle of liquor squares you for saving his life?"

"Well, he *is* Irish," she said. "Depends on the liquor."

Vic, caught off-guard, actually smiled a little. Then he scowled again. "I think maybe I'll stick with vodka."

"Shut up," Erin said. She opened a cabinet and pulled out a pair of glasses. "You're gonna learn about whiskey."

She got a corkscrew from the drawer by the sink and popped the cork. The familiar hot, fierce smell of good whiskey rose to meet her. "It's too bad he didn't give me a bottle of Glen D, though. It's even better than Jameson."

"That's the Dockerty-whatever the captain was talking about?" Vic asked. "The shit you've gotta be Scottish to pronounce?"

"Yeah," Erin said. "You want it straight up?"

"Rocks," Vic said. "I worked up a sweat today."

Erin opened the freezer and dropped two ice cubes into each glass. She loved the musical clink they made as they landed. She poured a double shot into each glass. The ice cracked as the liquid cascaded over the cubes.

"Docherty-Kinlochewe," she said, trying out the words. "Did I say it right?"

"How the hell do I know?" Vic said. "Get a little drunk, then see how it sounds."

"Drink enough of it, you don't care about the pronunciation," she laughed. She handed one of the drinks to him.

Vic raised the glass to his lips.

"Hold on," she said. "We should have a toast."

"To what?"

She thought about it. "To making it home," she said. "To winning one. And to some damn fine shooting."

"Cheers," Vic said. They touched glasses.

Erin was about to take a good slug of Jameson when it hit her. Carlyle knew her favorite whiskey. She ordered it nearly every time she was at the Corner. A publican didn't forget something like that.

"Wait!" she said, suddenly and sharply.

Vic froze with the glass halfway to his mouth. "You do know the point of having a drink is to drink it, right?" Then he saw the look in her eyes. "What's the matter?"

She glanced sidelong around the room. Rolf had finished his meal and was tracking something only he could smell. He disappeared into her bedroom, then came back again and stood by the front door, staring at it.

"Rolf's been following it," she murmured. "He's been trying to tell me. I didn't listen."

"Tell you what? What's he following?" Vic was baffled.

"Heartbreaker," she said, almost to herself.

"Erin, I'm gonna start drinking until you start making sense."

She put a hand on his glass, keeping it down. She stepped forward and whispered to him, as if she was afraid someone else might overhear. "I think I know how to get our serial killer," she said. "But I need your help."

She explained, quickly and quietly. Vic listened, at first surprised, then nodding his understanding. "Okay," he muttered. "We'll do it your way. But it's a waste of good Scotch if you're wrong."

*   *   *

Vic attached Rolf to his leash again. The Shepherd was confused, but was perfectly willing to go for another walk. He knew Vic and got on fine with him. But when Vic opened the door and stepped into the hallway, Rolf stayed put. He looked quizzically at Erin. She was supposed to go with him. That was the first rule of police work. You didn't leave your partner behind.

"It's fine, Rolf," Erin said. "*Geh rein.*"

Rolf permitted himself to be led away. Erin went to the door and fastened the deadbolt and chain lock. Then she took the bottle of Jameson and her whiskey glass to the dining table. She sat down at the table and stared at the amber liquid. Vic was right. It was a hell of a waste.

"Here goes," she muttered. She hoped her intuition was right.

About thirty seconds later, she got out of her chair. She stumbled, threw out a hand to the tabletop, missed, and collapsed to the floor. The glass hit the linoleum and shattered. Drops of whiskey spattered the ground.

Chapter 19

Some time passed, maybe five minutes. Then there was a knock at Erin's door. After a short pause, the knock was repeated.

Erin lay where she'd fallen. Her eyes were closed, her breathing shallow.

A key turned in the lock. It wasn't a perfect fit, but the lock opened with a little careful persuasion. The door came partway open and stopped, arrested by the chain. A hand slid into the space. The chain should've been short enough to keep a human arm from fitting through the gap, but this chain was just a little too long. The fingers, covered by a latex glove, deftly opened the night lock. The door swung open.

"Oh no," said a soft, polite male voice. "I hope you haven't hurt yourself. If you've cut that beautiful face, I'll never forgive either of us."

Erin made no response. She didn't move at all.

The intruder walked toward her. "I hope you liked the whiskey," he said. "It's a good brand, top-shelf. Almost three hundred dollars. But you deserve the best. I'm so sorry we have to do it this way, so rushed. I know we would both prefer to savor the experience. But your friend will be back soon."

"This isn't how I wanted it to be at all," he went on. He reached into his trouser pocket and took out a plastic disposable syringe. He took the cap off it and raised it to point toward the ceiling, tapping it like a nurse preparing to give a shot. "I'd like to undress you, look at you... but there's no time. You'll just have to know that I do appreciate your beauty, more than any other man ever could. And I hope you know that I love you very, very much."

He bent over her.

Erin opened her eyes. They were bright and alert, no trace of drugs or drowsiness. "Thank you, Trevor," she said. "That's the nicest thing anyone's said to me all day."

Trevor Fairfax froze in place, his face a mask of shock. He opened his mouth but no words came out.

"I only just figured it out," she said, standing up. "Of course, Rolf knew from the moment he smelled you outside the DoubleTree. Heartbreaker fragrance. You've got it all over you."

"I... I work in a perfume shop, Erin," Trevor said. "Of course I smell like perfume. I stopped by to see you. You didn't answer, so I came in to make sure you were all right."

"Through a locked door?" Erin said. "And a chain lock? Nice trick, by the way. A guy I know told me how you did it. You must have a skeleton key for the main lock. You came in with that earlier and swapped out the chain. Rolf tracked you in here, too. You broke into a detective's home. That's plenty for a warrant, and I'll bet once we look in your house—"

Trevor lunged at her, stabbing with the syringe.

Erin had been waiting for him to make his move. She lashed out with her leg, sweeping his feet out from under him. Shards of broken glass skittered across the floor. Trevor went down with a crash, the syringe flying from his hand.

He was quicker than she'd thought. He twisted like a snake and scrambled back to his feet. Erin reached for her gun. But Trevor wasn't a fighter. He spun and dashed for the door.

Even as he reached it, he skidded to a halt. Vic Neshenko stood there, his Sig Sauer automatic in one hand, Rolf's leash in the other.

"Hey, Erin?" Vic called past Trevor. "What's Rolf's bite command again?"

All the energy went out of Trevor. His legs folded up beneath him. He put his hands over his face. "No," he whimpered. "Don't let him bite me."

Vic stared at him with an expression of disgusted surprise. "Is he *crying?*"

Erin got out her cuffs. "Careful," she said. "He's clever."

"Don't worry," Vic said, keeping his pistol trained on the clerk. "He's not going anywhere. I've shot two guys today already. Want to make it a hat trick?"

"Trevor Fairfax," Erin said. "You're under arrest for breaking and entering, assaulting a police officer, attempting to murder a police officer, ruining a three-hundred-dollar bottle of Scotch, and murdering Janice Barnes. You have the right to remain silent..."

* * *

"This is not what I meant when I told you to go home," Webb said.

"He broke into my apartment," Erin said. "What was I supposed to do, let him go with a stern warning?"

They were back at the precinct, nowhere close to done with what promised to be a very late night. They'd booked Trevor and dropped him in a holding cell, then waited for their commanding officer to make his way back from Brooklyn. Neither Erin nor Vic had gotten their drink yet.

"I dunno," Vic said. "I could've let him past me. Rolf could use the exercise."

"You saying something about my dog?"

"He's looking a little pudgy, that's all I'm saying."

"That's it," Erin said. "I'm putting you back in the bite suit. And I'm spraying beef broth on the crotch before I do."

"Save the kinky stuff for when you're off-duty," Webb said. "But seriously, O'Reilly. How'd you know he was coming after you?"

"He sedated his victims with drugged wine," Erin said. "If he'd used a wine bottle on me, I would've figured it faster. He gave me whiskey instead, but it was still suspicious. Rolf acted funny when I had him do a search. He started tracking down the hall after he got a whiff of the bag.

"Vic and I didn't notice it right away, but that Heartbreaker fragrance is powerful and it lingers. I'd had Rolf tracking it earlier. He tried to alert to Fairfax when I ran into him outside the hotel. Fairfax pretended it was a chance meeting, and I was distracted enough that I didn't think too much of it, but he'd been following me. He tracked me from Corcoran's apartment. One of the O'Malleys' enforcers tipped me off that I had a tail. He can probably ID Fairfax."

"If he'll testify, which I doubt," Vic put in.

"Whatever," Erin said. "We don't need his testimony. Fairfax got into my apartment with a skeleton key. He wanted to case it so he'd be ready when he came in to get me. He fixed the night lock the same way he did with the hotel room, replacing the chain with one that was just a little longer. He must've looked through my liquor cabinet while he was there, to find out what I liked."

"A considerate serial killer," Webb muttered.

Erin snorted. "He probably really thinks so. The way he was talking when he came in, it was like he felt he'd form a real connection with me by killing me." She shook her head. "The sick bastard thinks he loves the women he kills."

"What else do we have on him?" Webb asked.

"I got the employment records from the DoubleTree," Erin said. She'd had time to check her e-mail while waiting for Webb to arrive. "Fairfax worked there, doing room service, when he was just out of high school. He couldn't duplicate the magnetic keys by himself, but the hotel has old-school keys for accessing their maintenance areas. He copied those while he worked there. Then he snuck in and grabbed a hotel uniform from the back. After that he could creep in any time and make copies of his victims' keycards."

"Victims," Webb said. "How many?"

"We'll know once we search his apartment," Erin said.

"We'll find trophies," Vic said.

"Exactly," Erin said. "I'm guessing it'll be photographs. His whole thing is about watching women. The bodies were never mutilated. He might have kept some of their clothes, too, but I think we'll find pictures. It may even help us close some other cases."

"How did he know you'd drink the whiskey when you did?" Webb asked.

"I didn't drink it," she reminded him.

"It's been too long a day for bullshitting," Webb said. "You know what I mean."

"The bottle wasn't there when I left home this morning," Erin said. "He staked out my place after delivering it, so he was waiting nearby. We pulled a smartphone off him when we took him in. The phone has an app that connects to those hidden cameras, like people use to check on their pets when they're at work."

"Or their cheating spouses," Vic added.

Erin shuddered at the memory of seeing her apartment on the screen of Trevor's phone. "He'd planted hidden cams in every room," she said. "Dining room, living room, bedroom, even the bathroom."

"Especially that," Vic growled. "That son of a bitch. We're not allowed to whack suspects with phone books anymore, are we?"

"Knock it off, Neshenko," Webb said. "So, he saw the two of you talking, then Neshenko leaving with Rolf. And then you took a drink and hit the floor."

"I don't know what he would've done if Vic had still been there," Erin said. "If he and I had both drunk, we'd have both gone down. He might've left Vic there, or he might've killed both of us. I know he'd have killed Rolf if he could."

"Because Rolf knew what he smelled like," Vic said.

"Yeah," Erin said. "I figured if we acted like Vic was just taking Rolf out for a quick walk, Fairfax would think he had a chance, but only if he moved fast. When perps are in a rush, they get sloppy. I was just lucky he didn't get his hands on my usual whiskey. That was what kept us from drinking."

Webb had Erin's case notes in front of him. While they talked, he'd been scanning them, taking in the contents. "Okay," he said. "Let's get him in the interrogation room. You don't need to be there for this."

Erin bristled. "Sir, this is my collar. You think I'm scared of him?"

Webb looked at her wearily. "I think this is going to be a shitty conversation with a genuine monster. It's going to be unpleasant in every way. Guys like this can get inside your head, and once they are, it's hard to get rid of them."

"I don't care what he does in my head," Erin said, "because I'll know where his body is. It'll be upstate in maximum security, because I put it there. You put me in charge of this case. Let me bring it home."

Webb's tired features cracked into a faint but unmistakable smile. "Damn right," he said. "Let's go put this one away."

* * *

In the hall outside the interrogation room, Webb paused. "O'Reilly," he said, "are you sure you're ready for this?"

"Of course."

"Fairfax has a thing about women."

"That's one way of putting it."

"We'll both be talking, but he'll be paying attention to you."

"That's what I'm counting on," she said.

"You want to be good cop or bad cop?"

She smiled grimly. "I'll be the good one."

"You arrested him," Webb reminded her.

"He'll see that as getting attention. It'll help."

"Okay, we'll try it your way," he said and opened the door.

Trevor sat at the table, hands folded on the tabletop, face calm. There was no sign of the whimpering and tears he'd turned on when Vic had threatened him. Erin wondered whether he'd had any genuine emotional reaction, or if emotions were something he put on like an extra layer of clothing. She only knew one thing that sparked genuine feeling in him. It was her job to play on that.

Trevor glanced at Webb, then turned his eyes toward Erin. There was sudden warmth in his gaze. It looked so genuine that it almost fooled her.

Webb grabbed the back of one of the empty chairs and deliberately scraped it across the floor with a grating shriek of metal. Trevor flinched a little but didn't otherwise react or take his eyes off Erin. Webb sat down and leaned forward, getting into Trevor's personal space.

"You're in deep shit, Fairfax," Webb growled. "No, don't look at her. Look at me!" He shifted sideways, blocking Trevor's line of sight. "Worry about me. Because your ass is mine, pencil-dick."

Trevor looked at Webb like he was a minor annoyance. "I'm sorry... who are you?"

"Lieutenant Webb, NYPD."

"Ah," Trevor said. "You'd be Erin's boss, then?"

"Detective O'Reilly to you," Webb snapped.

"You seem a little protective of her," Trevor said mildly. "Older man, getting a little out of shape... I notice you don't wear a wedding ring, but you used to. There's an indent in your ring finger."

Webb, despite himself, put his right hand over his left, unconsciously feeling his ring finger.

"Divorced, I suppose," Trevor went on. "Long hours on the job, no time for the family? Maybe bringing the job home with you, into your house... into your bedroom?"

"Screw you," Webb snarled. "I'm going to personally see to it that you go into Gen Pop with the worst batch of offenders I can find. They'll be cornholing you seven days a week, twice on Saturdays."

Trevor smiled slightly. He was making Webb lose his cool. That was putting him more in control of the situation.

"Trevor," Erin said, moving forward, getting back into his field of view. "Don't." She spoke quietly, deliberately contrasting with her commanding officer. "Please."

Trevor turned immediately away from Webb, looking straight into Erin's eyes. "I'm sorry," he said. "You shouldn't have to listen to filthy talk like that. This man has no idea of the proper way to talk in the presence of a lady."

"I'm used to it," Erin said.

"You shouldn't have to be," Trevor said earnestly. "You're better than that, Erin."

"Detective O'Reilly," Webb interjected.

"It's okay, sir," Erin said, holding up a hand. There was a science to two-officer interrogations. When trying to break two suspects, the police tried to drive a wedge between them, make them turn on each other. When dealing with one suspect, especially a smart one like this, the reverse could work. If they could make Trevor think he was dividing his captors, he'd keep talking. The worst thing that could happen in an interrogation was for a suspect to ask for a lawyer. The second worst was that he'd simply keep his mouth shut. A talking prisoner was a valuable prisoner.

Webb opened his mouth, then closed it and quietly fumed, hamming up his role.

"Trevor," she said. "I've been thinking about what you said, in my apartment. You said you appreciated me more than any other man could." She turned half away, feigning embarrassment.

He nodded. "It's true. You can't expect someone like the Lieutenant here, with his crude physicality, to really appreciate you. The way our society glorifies crass obscenity... it makes me sick. You're better than that. More pure."

She slowly looked back at him. "But I thought you wanted to... to touch me," she said. "Maybe even... rape me."

"Rape?" he echoed, looking genuinely horrified. "I could never do that to you, Erin." He shook his head violently. "I'm no rapist! How could you think that?"

"I'm sorry, Trevor," she said. "Help me understand. I'm used to men who only want one thing."

"Of course," he said. "Spending all your time among the filth of this city, you probably have to deal with all sorts of crude propositions, vile jokes, harassment. But I'm not like that. I love you, Erin. I... I worship you." His eyes were shining. He seemed to have completely forgotten Webb was even in the room.

Erin leaned closer to him, making her own eyes as bright and earnest as she could. "You want me," she said in a low, husky voice.

"Yes," Trevor whispered.

"You want to look at me," she went on, shifting her shoulder back slightly to call attention to her body.

"Yes," he said again. He licked his lips and stared hungrily at her.

"You want to dress me up in something beautiful."

"The black velvet," he said softly.

"The one in my closet?" she asked softly.

"Yes," he said. "You would be stunning."

"You could watch me sleep," she murmured, "for hours if you wanted to. And when you couldn't stand it any longer, you'd take that needle and push it gently into my arm."

Trevor was trembling. "It's amazing," he said hoarsely. "There's no pain. You shiver, shudder, and then you go deep, under the surface. Your face goes quiet and calm, all the worry and tiredness of the world falls away. And I capture you that way, forever."

"You'd take my picture?" she asked, lowering her head and looking up under her eyelashes at him. "And keep it? Forever?"

"Forever," he promised.

"With the others?"

"You'd be the best of them all."

"That ought to be good enough," Erin said, returning suddenly to her normal tone of voice. She stood up abruptly and pushed herself away from the table. She couldn't stand it any longer.

Trevor blinked, seeming to remember where he was. "What—" he began.

"Fuck you, Trevor Fairfax," Erin spat. "You're not even human. You're a monster. And a moron."

Webb stood up and smiled fiercely at the prisoner. "I thought it'd take a couple hours to crack you," he said. "A pretty detective bats her eyes at you, and you give it all up. She's right. You're dumber than I thought. You've given us plenty. When CSU searches your place, they'll know exactly what to look for. Come on, O'Reilly. We're done with this garbage."

They went to the door. As Webb opened it, Trevor stood up.

"Wait!" he shouted. "Erin! Don't listen to him! To them! I love you! I love—"

Erin slammed the door, cutting him off mid-sentence. Then she leaned her back against it and let out a long, shuddering breath.

She became aware of a sound. It was hands clapping. She looked up and saw Vic and half a dozen other officers who'd been watching from the observation room. They were applauding her.

Webb extended his hand. "Good work, Detective," he said. "You almost fooled me."

"That's an Oscar," Vic said. "Goddamn Academy Award."

"Thanks, guys," she said, shaking Webb's hand. "But Vic, I could really use that drink right now." And after that, she thought, a very long shower.

Chapter 20

Trevor Fairfax lived in a very ordinary apartment in Brooklyn Heights, just south of the East River. According to all their information, he lived alone. But under the circumstances, Webb was taking no chances. The detectives went in with guns drawn, clearing the apartment as carefully as if it'd been a drug den full of desperate gangsters.

It was anticlimactic. The one-bedroom third-floor walkup was neat, tidy, and deserted.

"Not much furniture," Vic observed, stepping out of the bathroom and looking around the living room. The furnishings were strictly of the IKEA sort, very plain. Trevor had a big-screen TV on one wall, but that was the only expensive piece.

"He likes photography," Kira said. She was looking at a bookcase full of books about cameras and photo technique. A table in the corner had a whole array of cameras and lenses neatly laid out.

"There's some nice stuff here," Webb said, bending to examine the equipment. "Good surveillance gear. We've got infrared."

Erin went into the bedroom, not without a shudder. She was expecting something terrifying. Stalker shrines weren't as common in police work as Hollywood wanted them to be, but they still happened. She was almost disappointed by what she found. All Trevor had was a bed with simple white sheets and comforter, a computer desk with a laptop, and a single photograph on the wall. It was a black-framed still life of a bouquet of red roses.

"Got a computer here," she called, flipping it open and powering it up with a gloved fingertip. It prompted her for a password, of course. She cursed under her breath. The NYPD had tech guys who could probably break in, but it'd take time. She turned it off again.

"Hey, Erin," Vic called. "You wanna come out here for a second?"

"What's up?" she asked, sticking her head through the doorway.

"We got some pics on the cameras," he replied. "And our boy's got a pretty sweet setup here. We can plug the camera right into the TV. We're gonna take a look, see what he's been taking pictures of lately."

"Okay," she said without much enthusiasm. Her skin was crawling. "Let's see what we've got."

"I have a bunch of tools in the front closet," Kira called. "And... whoa, got a uniform from the DoubleTree. Not looking good for our boy."

Vic hooked up a camera to the main screen. Webb stood behind the living-room couch, careful not to touch any of the furniture. Erin went to stand beside him, not sure what to expect.

She saw herself, in the park outside her apartment, holding Rolf's leash.

"Jesus," Vic muttered.

"Cycle the pics," Webb said. "O'Reilly, if you don't want to see this…"

"It's okay," she said through clenched teeth.

The next several pictures were all of Erin's face, gradually zooming in until she filled the whole screen. Erin tried to work out where Trevor had been standing while he took the shots. He'd been close, less than twenty yards away, probably behind one of the trees.

"What's that?" Webb asked, pointing.

"My phone," Erin said. "He… shit, he called me. He was on the phone with me while he took this."

"Jesus," Vic said again. "Lucky bastard."

"Lucky how?" Kira asked.

"Lucky we already have him in custody," he said. "Otherwise I'd kill the son of a bitch."

"You might have to get in line," Webb said dryly.

Erin said nothing, but she knew in her heart that if Vic had wanted to kill Trevor, he'd have had to get up early to get ahead of her.

The next picture was so dark, it took them all a second to figure out what it was.

"That's funny," Kira said. "This was taken indoors, without a flash, in a dark room. It looks like some sort of crowd shot."

Erin felt her legs go weak. She couldn't tell which was stronger in her, anger or horror. "It's a movie theater," she said in a flat, dead voice.

"Oh, right," Kira said. "Yeah, I see you in the frame, there. Must've been taken from the front row, aimed up."

Vic thumbed to the next shot. It was the same. So was the next.

"Who's that next to you, leaning on you?" Webb asked.

Erin's throat had a lump in it. She swallowed and licked her lips. "Anna," she managed to get out. "Anna O'Reilly. My niece."

No one said anything for maybe half a minute.

"Turn it off," Webb said finally. "We've seen enough."

Chapter 21

The Barley Corner didn't reopen right away. In addition to the usual red tape—and yellow police tape—surrounding the crime scene, there was the issue of the physical damage to the pub.

The smart thing would have been to stay away regardless. But Erin walked by the Corner six days after the shootout, as part of Rolf's after-work outing. She wasn't completely sure why she did. Curiosity, maybe. And she felt she ought to talk to Carlyle again.

CSU had cleared the building to do business, but the CLOSED sign still hung on the door. Erin stepped up close to a window and cupped her hands around her face, trying to see inside.

The door opened. Surprised, Erin stepped back.

"Erin, darling," Carlyle said, smiling. "An Irishwoman can't simply stand outside a public house."

"You're closed," she said.

"My door's always open for you," he said, extending a hand. "Come in, have a drink with me. Assuming you're off-duty, of course."

She and Rolf went in. Erin noticed that he locked the door behind her. The bar was looking much better than the last time she'd seen it. The scorched section of floor had been scraped and re-stained, the bullet holes filled in with spackle and painted over, and Carlyle's door replaced. A pair of workmen were putting the finishing touches on the floor repairs. Besides the workers, Carlyle, and Erin, the only other person in the place was a young man she recognized from the lobby of Corky's apartment. He was about twenty-five, with reddish-brown hair in a buzz cut. He wasn't very tall or heavily built, but was obviously in excellent condition. He wore a plain, dark sport coat and slacks over a dark green button-down shirt and black tie. The way he wore it, he made it look like a military uniform. Erin would've bet a week's pay he had a gun under his coat.

She nodded to the man. He politely returned the nod, then turned his attention to the outside.

"Looks like you're about ready for business again," she said to Carlyle.

"Aye," he said. "In point of fact, I'll be opening the doors later this evening, having a small celebration. Danny will be here in a little while, but for now, I'll be serving you myself. I hope you're not wanting any particularly complicated beverage. I fear my skill at tending bar is no match for his."

"No problem," she said. "I'll just have a Scotch. No, make it a double. On the rocks."

"House brand?" he asked, going behind the bar.

"Glen D," she confirmed.

"None but the finest," he said, setting two glasses on the bar and dropping ice cubes into them. He poured two generous double whiskeys, then came back around to her side of the bar and took a seat next to her, handing her one of the glasses. Rolf had lain down at her feet.

"Here's to you, Erin," he said, raising his glass.

She clinked her glass to his. They drank.

"From what I've seen in the papers, I understand you got your man," Carlyle said.

"Yeah, I did," she said. The hotel murders had made the headlines in a big way. The press had decided to call Trevor the Heartbreaker Killer, and the name seemed to have stuck. "We've got plenty of evidence. We cracked his computer. It was full of photographs."

"How many did he kill?"

"I can't tell you that," she said, reflecting again on the similarities between their jobs.

"Of course not. My apologies. I'm glad you've caught him."

"When I want to get a guy, I usually do, sooner or later."

"I don't doubt it," Carlyle said. "Here's hoping I never find myself on your bad side." He took another sip of Glen D.

"That's easy enough," she said. "Don't step out of line."

Carlyle smiled, a hint of melancholy in his eyes. "Things aren't always as simple as they're made to appear."

"So I'm learning. You helped me catch him, you know."

"I'm glad," Carlyle said. "That's a lad's civic duty."

She shook her head. "I'm still trying to figure you out. Sometimes you help me, sometimes you don't. What are we doing here?"

"We're sharing a quiet drink."

"I mean, why are we even talking? One of my squad reminded me you could get killed just for giving the appearance of talking to the NYPD."

"I'm not talking to the NYPD," Carlyle said. "I'm talking to you."

"Same thing."

"Is it?"

"To them it is. You know that better than I do."

"Aye, perhaps it is," Carlyle said. "But perhaps I've decided it's worth the risk."

"What is?"

"Being able to call you a friend."

"So that's what we are?" Erin said, raising her eyebrows. "Seems a little dangerous, for both of us. Come to think of it, I'm a little surprised. I've been here five whole minutes already, and nobody's tried to blow the place up yet."

"I've made some improvements to my personal security," Carlyle said.

Erin cocked her head toward the young man. "That the guy who tipped you off that Fairfax was following me?"

"Aye," Carlyle said. "Ian's a good lad and quite observant. I think he'll go far."

"So Ian's there to make sure you don't get killed for having a friend who carries a shield," she said. "This is one crazy world you live in."

Carlyle chuckled. "Aye. But it's my home."

"You know," Erin said, "they're still dragging the East River. So far the diving teams have come up with two John Does, and one Jane Doe, but no sign of Rüdel's body."

"Are you saying he survived?"

"I dunno," Erin said. "Vic tagged him pretty good. I don't think he made it, but until we come up with a body, that case stays open. That means I need to keep an eye on the O'Malleys."

"Why would you draw such a conclusion?"

She leaned in and lowered her voice. "Come on, Carlyle, you know damn well it was one of your own people who sent him after you."

"I said no such thing," Carlyle said.

"No," Erin said, slowly and distinctly. "You didn't."

"You're a very fine detective. Has anyone told you that lately?"

"You wanted me to find Rüdel," she said, still speaking quietly. "And you do know who sent him after you."

"If what you're saying is true," he said, "you surely understand why I'd not be giving you a name. Besides, your lads are held to a standard of evidence beyond what I'd be able to provide in such a case."

She looked him in the eye. "You're saying this is your problem and you're going to deal with it in your own way, is that right?"

"I believe a man's duty in this world is to clean up his own messes."

"And a woman's duty is to clean up the shit left behind by stupid men," Erin countered.

Carlyle laughed. "I'll not disagree with you there. But why concern yourself with such things?"

"If you go to war with another of the O'Malleys, it becomes my business," she said. "If bodies start dropping, that's gonna come across my desk sooner or later. I don't want to have to arrest you."

"Here's where you add that you will if you have to, aye?" Carlyle said. He was smiling as he said it, but it was a surprisingly gentle smile.

"If you make me," she said. "It's your call. Major Crimes doesn't come after you unless you give us a reason."

"But you truly don't want to."

"No," she said, "I don't."

"May I ask why?"

Erin paused. She'd blurted out the truth without really thinking about it. And too much truth was sometimes a dangerous thing. But she was finally starting to understand Morton Carlyle, and she knew on a gut level that she wasn't in danger from him, at least not directly.

She decided to risk a little more truth. "You're gonna think this is crazy," she said. "Hell, I think it's crazy. I wear a shield, you... God, we're supposed to be enemies. But I feel like you understand me better than anyone else in this damn city. There's things we can't say, but we say more without actually saying anything... shit, do you know what I mean?"

He nodded. "Aye, Erin, I do."

"That's exactly what I'm talking about," she said. "I like being able to talk to you, even when you piss me off."

"Likewise."

"When have I ever pissed you off?" she demanded.

"You did wrongfully accuse me of murder once," he reminded her.

"That bounced right off you! You just smiled and ordered a drink, then drank it right in front of me!"

"Fair enough, darling," Carlyle said. "Nay, you're right, I've not yet been truly angry with you. You've given me more than a fair shake, and that's all a lad can ask."

She shook her head in quiet wonder. "We really are friends."

"I hope so."

"How'd this happen?"

"I suppose defusing a bomb together is a bit of a test for that sort of thing," he said.

It was Erin's turn to laugh. "Yeah, I guess so. Remember Corky standing there, afraid to move?"

"And him flirting with you all the while," Carlyle chuckled. "I swear, when the Grim Reaper comes for Corky, he'll ask the bony old lad if he's been on a diet, because he's looking fantastic."

"I also remember your first reflex," she said.

"What do you mean?"

"I mean you put yourself between me and a live bomb."

"Oh, you needn't dwell on that," he said. "I was throwing myself to the floor and met you on the way down."

"And I just happened to be in the way?"

"Always the detective, aren't you, Erin? Here we are, having a pleasant conversation, and I've the feeling you're trying to get me to admit to something."

"I'm trying to get you to admit that the life-saving hasn't just gone one way."

"I didn't save your life."

"If that bomb had gone off, you might've."

"Do you live your life on the basis of hypotheticals?"

"I swear to God, you're the hardest man in New York to pin down," she said. "I know I said I understood you, but there's limits."

"Now I think it's my turn to try to get you to admit to something," he said.

"What's that?"

"You like trying to puzzle me out."

"Yeah," she said. "Maybe I do."

"Then to be fair, here's an admission from me."

"Really? No ducking and dodging?"

"Not this time."

"I can't wait to hear this," she said. "Fire away."

"I appreciate your honesty," he said. "You say what you believe, and you don't shy from it. That's a rare thing in this world, rarer still in my little corner of it."

She didn't know what to say to that, so she just said, "Thanks."

"And now I'd like to propose another toast," he said, lifting his glass.

"To what?"

"To mystery."

She touched her glass to his. "And to finding the answers."

"But not too soon," he said. "That would spoil all the fun."

Here's a sneak peek from Book 5: Manhattan

Coming 2019

Erin's phone buzzed in her pocket. She started, then fished it out, feeling a little silly for her nerves. She saw the name of her commanding officer on her caller ID and sighed. Lieutenant Webb didn't make courtesy calls.

She thumbed her screen. "O'Reilly."

"Where are you?" Webb asked. No small talk, straight to the point.

"At a bar."

"Not drunk, are you?"

"No, sir. Just had one."

"Okay, get back here right now."

"Sure thing." She pushed back from the bar and hopped off the stool. Rolf jumped up and followed. "What's up?"

"A 10-13 just came over the net."

Erin didn't understand. The code for an officer needing assistance was important, sure, but they wouldn't rope in an off-duty detective for it. There were literally thousands of Patrol officers who could respond more quickly. "I'll get there as quick as I can, but—"

He cut her off. "It's too late for that. An officer's down."

Her heart lurched. "We got units on scene?"

"Yeah," Webb said. But she already knew from his tone what he was going to say. "We lost him."

She didn't want to ask the next question, but she had to know. "Who is it?"

Webb hesitated a second too long. She felt like she was going to throw up. Names chased each other through her brain.

"He's from our precinct," he said. "It's Hendricks, one of the rookies. Bob Michaelson's partner."

Erin had to stop moving for a second and close her eyes. "What happened?"

"We're detectives, O'Reilly. It's our job to find that out."

* * *

The scene of the shooting was just off FDR Drive, near the East River. A full squadron of NYPD cruisers was deployed on Fletcher Street, under FDR. Grim-faced uniformed officers were everywhere. There were even half a dozen guys in full ESU tactical gear, assault rifles in their hands.

The other members of Erin's squad were already there. Vic Neshenko gave her a curt nod. Kira Jones looked at Erin with haunted eyes.

"Hey, Erin," Kira said quietly.

"Hey," Erin replied, unable to think of anything else to say.

"I heard they pushed you up to Second Grade," Vic said to Erin by way of greeting.

"Yeah." She hadn't wanted to bring it up. Vic was still a Detective Third Grade, and she wasn't sure how he felt about her being promoted over his head.

"Suppose that means you're gonna be looking for more respect."

"No, I expect you'll still be an asshole."

"Okay. No problem, then."

If Vic ever went to prison, he'd never get time off for good behavior, but Erin still liked him. However surly he got, he was rock solid when things went sideways. There was no man in the NYPD she'd prefer to have watching her back.

"How long had Hendricks been wearing his shield?" she wondered aloud.

"The hell would I know? I guess maybe he was with the last Academy class."

"Jesus," Erin said. "On the Job less than a year."

"It's always the newbies that get it," he said. "They can't read the street yet."

"Their training officers are supposed to keep them alive," she said.

"Yeah," Vic said. "What the hell was Michaelson doing, letting this happen? He's been around longer than God."

"I'll bet Michaelson's asking himself the same thing," Erin said. She was thinking of John Brunanski, the officer who'd died holding her hand. She still thought about what she could've, should've done differently, all the ways she could've saved him.

"Hell of a thing," Vic said.

"Yeah."

"Okay, team," Webb said. "We're all thinking it. This is a shitty situation. But every case we get is shit. They don't call Major Crimes over parking tickets. Let's work the case and get it solved."

The crime scene was obvious. A squad car was angled across the narrow street, both front doors standing open. The detectives gathered around the car and stared. The passenger-side window had three bullet holes in it, tightly grouped. Blood was spattered on the door panel and pooled on the pavement. Discarded bits of packaging for first-aid supplies were strewn around. There was no body.

"Where's Hendricks?" Webb asked the nearest uniform.

"I heard they took him to Bellevue," the officer replied.

"Small world," Erin muttered. Her oldest brother was a trauma surgeon there.

"What's that, Detective?" the patrolman asked.

"Nothing," she said.

Bob Michaelson was sitting on the curb a little ways off. He was a heavyset Patrol sergeant in his mid-forties. Here, today, he looked twice that old. The other officers had given Michaelson some respectful space, so he sat all alone. He was covered with blood. Hands, face, uniform. Someone had put a paper cup of coffee in his hand. He didn't seem to have noticed it.

"Poor guy," Kira said softly.

Webb sighed. "Let's get this over with." They walked to stand in front of Michaelson. He didn't look up.

Webb cleared his throat. "Excuse me, Sergeant."

Michaelson raised his head. He looked straight through Webb.

"What happened, Bob?" Webb asked, his voice surprisingly gentle.

"Normal patrol," Michaelson said. He sounded hoarse, like a man who'd smoked too many cigarettes. "Same shit, different day. We came down Maiden Lane. I saw that door," he waved a hand indifferently toward the building behind him, "and spotted a possible forced entry."

Erin looked over Michaelson's shoulder. Sure enough, the warehouse at his back had a door that was standing ajar. She could see splintered wood on the doorframe, probably from a crowbar.

"Tim called it in," Michaelson went on. "I parked across Fletcher. Just then, the break-in crew came out."

"Carrying anything?" Webb asked.

"Duffel bags and handguns," Michaelson said. "Three suspects. Tim wanted to bust them right there, but I got an ID on their leader. I told Tim to call for backup, to fall back. But the kid wanted the collar. You know how rookies are. He was out of the car before I could stop him. He didn't listen." The old sergeant put a hand over his face. "I told him to get back in the car. He didn't listen."

"Bob," Webb said, "you know who the shooter was?"

He nodded. "I got a great look at his face. But it happened so goddamn *fast*. Bastard had his gun out the second Tim yelled 'NYPD!' I was still getting out my side of the car. The son of a bitch put three through the window there. Tim didn't even get a shot off, caught two right... right in the throat."

"Holy shit," Vic said softly. He was looking at the car door, tracing bullet trajectories with his fingertip. "That's some damn good shooting."

"Bob," Webb said again, "who the hell did this?"

Michaelson finally met Webb's eye. "Hans Rüdel."

*   *   *

"No."

Erin and Vic said it simultaneously. They glanced at one another, then back at Michaelson.

"That's not possible," Erin said.

"Rüdel's dead," Vic said. "That's not rumor, it's a goddamn fact. I put two bullets in his chest. I watched him go into the East River."

"I was there," Erin said. "I saw it too."

"Then he's got a twin brother," Michaelson said. "Because I just watched him put two through my partner's throat."

"You're sure it was him?" Erin pressed.

"He was seven, eight yards away. His face was all over the news last summer. Yeah, I'm sure."

Corky and Carlyle's behavior suddenly made sense to Erin. Rüdel had tried to kill Carlyle and nearly succeeded. If Corky had heard he was back in circulation, the two Irishmen had a very big problem.

Vic abruptly walked away from the damaged squad car. He went around the corner of the warehouse and out of sight. Webb and Kira were still talking to Michaelson, but Erin didn't think they'd find out much more. She and Rolf went after Vic.

She rounded the corner just in time to see the big Russian slam his hand against the brickwork. He pulled back his arm and did it again, then a third time. As she came cautiously toward him, he clenched his fists and let out one word.

"Fuck!"

Erin put out a hand and touched his shoulder. "Hey, Vic," she said. "Breathe, big guy."

He leaned against the wall with both hands, letting his head hang down between his shoulders. "I missed," he said.

"No you didn't," she said. "I was there. You nailed him twice."

"Should've made it three. Should've put one right in his damn face. He was right there, he was wounded, we had him! We were so goddamn sure he was dead, we didn't look that hard. And now that kid's dead. Because of me."

"Knock it off!" Erin snapped. "You are so full of shit. Hendricks is dead because we've got the most dangerous job in New York. He got careless and eager and he screwed up. You didn't make him get out of that car. You're blaming yourself, Michaelson's blaming himself, the only reason Hendricks isn't blaming himself is that he's not alive to do it. Will you lay off the self-pity so we can get some work done?"

Vic looked at her, and for a moment she was ashamed of herself when she saw the raw pain in his eyes. But it was only for a second. Then he locked it away in some deep, dark part of himself. He blinked, and when his eyes opened again his game face was on.

"You can be a cold, hard bitch, you know that?" he said.

"Had a lot of punks tell me that over the years," she replied.

"You know I love you for it."

"You getting mushy on me now?"

His lips moved in a grim parody of a smile. "Okay, tell me one thing. How the hell do we find this bastard?"

Erin hadn't been thinking of much else. "First we need his motive."

"That's easy. He didn't want to go to prison."

"No, not why he shot Hendricks. I mean, why was he breaking into this building in the first place?"

Vic thumped the bricks and winced.

"You okay?" Erin asked.

He studied his hand. Lines of blood streaked his palm. "Yeah, I'm fine."

"Better put on some gloves before we check the scene," she said. "Let's find out what Rüdel stole."

*   *   *

They couldn't just go inside. The Fourth Amendment, and the Supreme Court, dictated that the police needed a warrant unless they could show imminent danger to life or risk of destruction of evidence. Neither of those stipulations applied in this case, so they had to jump through the bureaucratic hoops. The silly thing was, everyone knew they'd get the warrant, but they still couldn't go in until they had it. Sillier still, they couldn't contact the owner of the warehouse.

"The lease is under the name Jameson," Kira said after some quick digging through a squad-car computer. "But I think it's a front. There's a phone number, but it goes to generic voicemail."

"We don't need the owner's permission," Webb said. "But it sounds like they're into something shady."

"Surprise," Vic muttered. "What, did you think he was stealing jelly beans?"

"Got the warrant," Kira announced.

"Okay," Webb said. "It's unlikely any of Rüdel's guys are still inside, but let's exercise some caution. Guns out, people."

They roped in a couple of ESU operators to help, just in case. The tactical guys lined up with the detectives outside. Webb cleared his throat.

"This is the NYPD! We're coming in to execute a search warrant. Anyone in there, keep your hands where we can see them!"

Vic and one of the ESU went first. Erin, Rolf, and another ESU guy followed. Webb and Kira brought up the rear with a small posse of NYPD uniforms. They moved quickly to clear the kill-zone in the doorway. The door itself was already broken and posed no obstacle.

Erin was tense and keyed up, ready for anything. She reminded herself to check her corners, to keep her field of fire clear. She could feel the nervous energy in her fellow officers. They were looking for some payback for Hendricks.

Vic was a big guy, and so was the ESU man beside him. All Erin could really see to her front was their shoulders and the backs of their heads and vests. When they suddenly stopped, just a few feet inside, she nearly ran into Vic's backside.

"Freeze!" Vic shouted. "Hands up!"

There was a momentary pause. Erin sidestepped, keeping partially obscured behind Vic's bulk. She brought her Glock in line and peered around him. Then she saw that she hadn't really been ready for anything.

A gorgeous redhead sitting calmly on a packing crate hadn't entered into her predictions for how this search was likely to go.

The woman looked to be in her mid- to late-twenties. She was dressed in dark, tight bluejeans and a black leather jacket that was open in front, showing a black turtleneck tight enough to show a fantastic figure. Her hair was a coppery auburn and was pulled back in a ponytail that made her look younger than she probably was. Her face was oval-shaped with high cheekbones. Her eyes were bright, penetrating green.

The woman slowly showed her hands to the police. She stood up, unhurried, ignoring the guns pointed her way. Then she smiled.

Erin saw something predatory in the expression. It was a fierce look, and she almost expected the woman's lips to draw back from her teeth.

The red-haired woman said, "Easy on those triggers, lads. You wouldn't want to be doing something we'd all regret, would you?"

Erin started at the unmistakable brogue of Northern Ireland. The woman could've come from the same neighborhood as Corky and Carlyle.

"What's your name, ma'am?" Vic demanded. He was still aiming his Sig-Sauer at her and seemed totally unimpressed with her feminine charms.

"Siobhan Finneran, lad," she said. "You're a bit tight-wound, aren't you. What do you call yourself, big fellow?"

"Detective Neshenko," Vic said. He, Erin, and one of the ESU guys moved in on her while the rest of the police spread out to finish clearing the warehouse.

"I'm Detective O'Reilly," Erin added.

Siobhan turned her attention to Erin, who caught a flicker of surprise in her eyes. Surprise, and maybe even recognition. Erin tried to remember whether she'd ever met Siobhan before. She was sure she wouldn't have forgotten someone so striking.

"O'Reilly?" Siobhan said. "Another Irishwoman. Oh, that's grand." There was something sardonic in her voice.

"Are you carrying any weapons, Ms. Finneran?" Vic asked.

"That depends on one's definition."

"Guns, knives, sharp objects," he said, refusing to flirt.

"Oh no, nothing of that sort."

"We need to check you anyway," he said. "Erin here can do it if you're not comfortable with a man—"

"You needn't worry about my tender feelings," she said. "Or are your doubting your self-control?"

"I'll do it," Erin said to preempt whatever retort Vic was brewing up. "Please extend your arms to either side, ma'am."

"Ma'am," Siobhan said, almost snorting. "I believe you're old enough to be my mother, or perhaps my aunt." She obeyed, but as Erin began patting her down, she looked the policewoman over. Erin felt like the search was a mutual thing. She didn't like it.

"You're not as pretty as I thought," Siobhan said in a quieter tone.

"Do I know you?" Erin asked.

"Oh no, marm," Siobhan said. "I'd remember."

Erin ran her hands over the other woman's shoulders and down her sides, repeating the basic frisking procedure she'd done dozens of times on patrol. Then she felt something and stopped. There was definitely a bulge under Siobhan's left arm.

"Ms. Finneran," Erin said, speaking with deliberate slowness, not wanting to startle anyone into rash action. "What have you got under your jacket?"

"It's a holster," Siobhan said.

"Whoa there," Vic said. "You said you weren't armed!"

"I'm not," she said. "It's simply a holster, no revolver in it. Feel free to check."

Erin wasn't about to take the woman at her word. She flipped back the leather jacket and saw it was true. Siobhan was wearing a shoulder holster, but it was empty.

"Where's the gun?" Erin asked.

"What gun?" Siobhan replied.

"Your gun."

"You can see I've no gun on my person. I'm breaking no laws."

We'll see about that, Erin thought and almost said out loud. What she did say was, "We're still going to need you to come with us and answer some more questions."

"Am I under arrest?"

"Only if you refuse."

Siobhan smiled icily. "An Irishwoman doesn't make idle threats."

Erin gave a cold smile of her own. "If I threaten you, Ms. Finneran, you'll know it."

They glared at each other for a long moment. Erin knew the other woman didn't like her, and that it was something that went beyond her being a police officer, but she didn't understand what it could be. Maybe she'd arrested Siobhan's brother, or lover, or something. Whatever it was, Siobhan was giving her the sort of look that on the street usually meant a fight was going to be on in a few seconds.

Kira saw it too. She interposed herself between the other two women. "I'll escort Ms. Finneran to the precinct," she said. "Why don't you and Rolf case the scene, make sure we don't miss anything?"

"Right," Erin said. As she turned away, she paused. "Make sure you check her for powder residue."

"Will do," Kira said.

"Oh aye, that's exactly the sort of thing a lass might do," Siobhan said. "Engage in a bit of pistol-play, then simply hang about the place waiting for the coppers. If I had bloody rocks in my head, maybe that's what I'd have done, but perhaps I'd simply have joined your police department instead."

Erin let the cheap shot pass. "Rolf," she said to her K-9, "*such.*"

It was his search command, spoken in his native German. The Shepherd put his nose to the ground and started sniffing. He was trained to search for humans, both living and dead, and explosives. She'd know what he found by his reaction. He scratched and whined when he located a person. If he smelled a bomb, he sat perfectly still and stared at it. Trainers had learned long ago that a dog pawing at an explosive device wasn't the best idea.

"We're clear," one of the ESU guys announced. The warehouse was half-full of packing crates and forklift palettes. There was a small office with an adjoining restroom, along with a maintenance room and a couple of empty side rooms. The police had checked all of these and found them vacant.

Erin wasn't expecting Rolf to find anything, but the Shepherd proved her wrong. He pulled toward the middle of one of the rows of boxes, then abruptly stopped and sat.

She took a look. Two big packing crates had been smashed open, probably with the same crowbar that had been used on the door. Their contents were jumbled, as if someone had rifled them in a quick search. It looked like they contained wool blankets.

"What've you got?" Vic asked, coming up behind her.

Erin had gone very cold inside. "I think he found what he was looking for," she said.

"What's that?"

She hoped like hell she was wrong. "Bombs."

Ready for more?

Join Steven Henry's author email list
for the latest on new releases, upcoming books and
series, behind-the-scenes details, events, and more.

Be the first to know about new releases in the Erin
O'Reilly Mysteries by signing up at
tinyurl.com/StevenHenryEmail

About the Author

Steven Henry learned how to read almost before he learned how to walk. Ever since he began reading stories, he wanted to put his own on the page. He lives a very quiet and ordinary life in Minnesota with his wife and dog.

Also by Steven Henry

Ember of Dreams
The Clarion Chronicles, Book One

When magic awakens a long-
forgotten folk, a noble lady, a young
apprentice, and a solitary blacksmith
band together to prevent war and seek
understanding between humans and
elves.

Lady Kristyn Tremayne – An otherwise unremarkable young lady's open
heart and inquisitive mind reveal a
hidden world of magic.

Robert Blackford – A humble harp
maker's apprentice dreams of being a hero.

Master Gabriel Zane – A master blacksmith's pursuit of perfection
leads him to craft an enchanted sword, drawing him out of his
isolation and far from his cozy home.

Lord Luthor Carnarvon – A lonely nobleman with a dark past has
won the heart of Kristyn's mother, but at what cost?

Readers love *Ember of Dreams*

*"The more I got to know the characters, the more I liked them. The female lead in
particular is a treat to accompany on her journey from ordinary to
extraordinary."*

*"The author's deep understanding of his protagonists' motivations and keen eye
for psychological detail make Robert and his companions a likable and
memorable cast."*

Learn more at tinyurl.com/emberofdreams.

More great titles from Clickworks Press

www.clickworkspress.com

Hubris Towers: The Complete First Season

Ben Y. Faroe & Bill Hoard

Comedy of manners meets comedy of errors in a new series for fans of Fawlty Towers and P. G. Wodehouse.

"So funny and endearing"

"Had me laughing so hard that I had to put it down to catch my breath"

"Astoundingly, outrageously funny!"

Learn more at clickworkspress.com/hts01.

The Altered Wake

Megan Morgan

Amid growing unrest, a family secret and an ancient laboratory unleash long-hidden superhuman abilities. Now newly-promoted Sentinel Cameron Kardell must chase down a rogue super-human who holds the key to the powers' origin: the greatest threat Cotarion has seen in centuries – and Cam's best friend.

"Incredible. Starts out gripping and keeps getting better."

Learn more at clickworkspress.com/sentinel1.

Death's Dream Kingdom
Gabriel Blanchard

A young woman of Victorian London has been transformed into a vampire. Can she survive the world of the immortal dead— or perhaps, escape it?

"The wit and humor are as Victorian as the setting... a winsomely vulnerable and tremendously crafted work of art."

"A dramatic, engaging novel which explores themes of death, love, damnation, and redemption."

Learn more at clickworkspress.com/ddk.

Share the love!

Join our microlending team at
http://www.kiva.org/team/clickworkspress.

Keep in touch!

Join the Clickworks Press email list
and get freebies, production updates, special deals,
behind-the-scenes sneak peeks, and more.

Sign up today at clickworkspress.com/join.

CPSIA information can be obtained
at www.ICGtesting.com
Printed in the USA
LVHW011959070119
603018LV00011B/311/P

FEB 1 5 2019